SPIRITUALLY MENTORING TEENAGE BOYS

PERSONAL DIALOGUE TO MAKE YOUNG SAINTS

FR MATTHEW P. SCHNEIDER, LC

ISBN: 0983541825
ISBN-13: 978-0983541820

DEDICATION

Dedicated to every boy you will mentor, that he may become a saint!

CONTENTS

Acknowledgements

First of all I need to thank Jesus Christ for forgiving all my sins and coming to me each day in the Eucharist. I want to thank Mary whose embrace I await in heaven.

I am on the front as the author, but this book is a huge collaborative effort. I need to thank the following people for forming me or helping me form myself: my parents Paul and Sheila, Daniel Beateau, Liem Tran OP, Julio Martí LC, and so many others who helped in other ways.

Thanks to the following people who helped me with stories, ideas and editing: Kevin Gore LC, Lucio Boccacci LC, Matthew DeGoede, Todd Brechbill, Daniel Brandenburg LC, Aaron Loch LC, David Murray, Hoa Nguyen LC, Daniel Turski, Jim Demboski, William Brock LC, Dave Monsour, Mark Haydu LC, my sisters (Amanda, Lee Ann, and Jenny), and the consecrated women of Regnum Christi. All the stories in this book are based on fact but names and personal details have been changed so as to protect identity. Mentoring is confidential.

INTRODUCTION

Mary stands, watching beneath the cross. "Flesh of my flesh, heart of my heart," she ponders. She looks up at her son then over at her companions. "The few," She says to herself. "Hundreds had followed Jesus. They had welcomed him into Jerusalem, but where are they now?"

Jesus' voice pierces through her silent thoughts. Then he breathes his last. Mary grabs the hands of her two companions, Mary Magdalene and John. These three stand more alone and yet more united than any three in history.

These are the only three disciples at the cross who we know anything about. Peter and the others were in hiding. What makes them different?

One difference seems to be that each of them had a personal experience of Jesus. We can imagine Mary's reaction when Jesus came home from carpentry and gave her a big hug. John calls himself "the disciple whom Jesus loved" and remembered a lot of personal details about Jesus that the other evangelists left out. Mary Magdalene felt personal forgiveness not as just something general. Others followed Jesus because he was the Messiah, because he did miracles, or because he was popular, but these three followed him because he was Jesus.

To be faithful to Jesus we need a personal relationship with him. We need to learn to speak with him one-on-one. Everyone heard what Jesus said, but these three understood him because of their personal experience. So often in Catholic youth ministry we focus almost exclusively on the group. The Gospel, however, shows Jesus worked with individuals too. Individual formation – which I call mentoring – can often be the most fruitful work with teens.

I, the author, am a member of the Legionaries of Christ, and most of my experience in youth ministry and mentoring is in Conquest clubs which are powered by ECyD. The principles I present can be applied to all Catholic youth ministry but I inevitably give my exposition a certain flavor. In this ministry, I've used mentoring extensively; some other youth ministries may apply it in a more limited fashion.

What Will We See?

This book is only meant to be an introduction. It cannot be all-encompassing, but rather, it is a foundation for the theoretical and practical aspects of mentoring. It is my own method and reflections – most of what I say is not dogma but one possible method. If you are already an expert as some area (you work professionally with teens or you are a spiritual director) please bear with me or skim the appropriate parts. There are dozens of books on prayer and adolescent psychology for continuing formation; unfortunately, there are few books specifically on forming adolescents into saints.

I am going to try to cover a lot of material in just a few short pages. I have tried to keep it short and save you unnecessary reading but I cannot guarantee it has been done perfectly. I take personal responsibility for any errors. We begin our roller coaster ride with some basics: why mentor, who can mentor, where should it happen, and what is it. The next section deals with an adolescent from philosophical, psychological, formational, and pedagogical perspectives (one at a time). After that comes a section on prayer and spirituality.

Finally, we sum all this up with a section of practical counsels.

Before moving on to the first chapter, let me tell the story of one Christian leader, Brian Bisgrove. After discerning a vocation several years and realizing God was not calling him to be a priest, Brian started a bunch of youth clubs to help boys become Christian men. The clubs he began are the beginning of what Conquest is today. Only a few years later, he was diagnosed with cancer. He went into the hospital but refused to take pain killers. The doctor tried to convince him but Brian said: "Go out in the hall and look at the crucifix – then come back in and tell me to take them." The doctor couldn't insist. Brian offered all his sufferings up for the boys in his clubs. He died in 1998.

About 10 years later, I asked his father what Brian would want to tell men who mentor boys, he handed over a copy of Brian's funeral card and pointed to Brian's own words: *"To know the will of God is the greatest knowledge, To find the will of God is the greatest discovery, And to do the will of God is the greatest achievement."* That phrase is a summary of the goal we seek in this book. If you are ready to begin the journey towards saint-making with teenage boys, let's begin.

MENTORING IN GENERAL

The title of each chapter in this section is a question. It's a mentoring FAQ of sorts. Each question takes a few pages to answer but with these answers, you should understand the basics of mentoring.

1. WHY MENTORING?

Recently, a high school friend sent me a friend request on Facebook. I hadn't heard from him since grade 12. It turns out he's spent the last decade working at a grocery store and playing bridge. He was one of the highest ranked young bridge players in Canada when we were in high school but he never got a break that would let him earn money off this passion. Worse, it turns out he's become a materialist. He can't escape the argument that the will is pre-determined. We often debated philosophy but when I left, nobody else was there to help him. The 3rd member of our small group of friends left Catholicism for Mormonism right after high school because a priest told his mom something horrendous.

They are not alone; today the Church is losing many teens. The Church has the truth but it's not being transmitted in a way teens can grasp. Mentoring has been absent from most Catholic youth ministry while at the same time mounting evidence suggests it's essential if we want teens to take on their faith as their own. Mentoring will help teens stay Catholic. Moreover, it will form the Christian leaders of tomorrow's world.

When it comes to helping teens stay Catholic, a whole slew

of research in recent years shows how important personal relationships (in general) and spiritual mentoring (specifically) are to maintain the faith. Many have shown this directly, and a few have shown this by showing the importance of a personal faith. I'm going to go through a bunch of arguments; if you already agree it may seem like I'm belaboring the point. I present them all because mentoring is absent many places it should be today. First let's examine why it's needed to keep teens Catholic then why it's needed to go deeper and disciple teens.

Middle school through college is the key to maintaining one's faith; let's examine this before we get to the studies showing how mentoring is key for remaining Catholic. The Pew Research Center[1] studied those who have changed religious affiliation and found that over 70% of those who leave the Catholic Church do so before age 24. This means if a young man stays Catholic from middle school through college, the chance he will leave the Church is minimal. Even good mentoring for a few of these years can give him the spiritual strength to stay Catholic for life.

Six recent books from different perspectives have shown the value of personal relationships with adults, and specifically spiritual mentoring, for teenage boys. They all point in the same direction even though terminology varies. I want to summarize all six here, even though that's a lot of material, to show how many different strands of research all point towards the need for spiritual mentoring to maintain the faith. '

In *Teen 2.0*, Robert Epstein (a secular Jew and psychologist) argues that to mature better and not be stuck unnecessarily long as children, teens need to have meaningful relationships with non-parental adults.[2] He points to Churches and Synagogues as the best place to start because it is the institution that is not segregated by age. Instead, we are all together for the celebration so it would seem natural we might talk a little afterwards. Allen and Allen reach similar conclusions in *Escaping Endless Adolescence*. They add, however, how little time – usually 20 minutes or less – is needed from non-parental adults to make a lasting effect on teens.[3]

Sociologist Christian Smith makes several related points in *Soul Searching*, the largest study of American teen religiosity to date. He points out that most teens want to be taught about God and not just entertained with religion. (Mentoring should teach them not only who God is but how he affects *their* life). He also notes that a teen's religiosity is related to how many adults other than his parents, such as mentors, a teen feels he can open up with or turn to for support.[4] After parents, other adults, like mentors, are one of the most important influences on teens' religiosity.

Sticky Faith studied what helped college kids from youth groups keep their faith and agreed with adult involvement in three ways. "By far, the number one way churches made the teens in our survey feel welcomed and valued was when adults in the congregation showed an interest in them."[5] Second, surveying high school seniors about their youth group experience what they most wanted was "time for deep conversation." And finally, "the students who feel most free to express doubts and discuss personal problems with youth leaders ... show more Sticky Faith."[6] Mentoring implies an adult taking interest in this particular teen and it is a key moment for deep conversation, both in general and, even more importantly, regarding his personal issues. It is a place he can bring up and discuss his doubts. It is unlikely a teen will be able to express personal doubts or have a deep conversation about personal issues in many places aside from mentoring.

You Lost Me paints the picture of the religious experiences of American teens and young adults. David Kinnaman focuses his research on 18 to 29-year-olds who grow up in a Christian environment. His approach is ministerial and retrospective rather than sociological and current like Smith's. Like Smith, he points out the importance of intergenerational relationships; however, he focuses on depth, not just numbers. He points out that only 12% of Catholic teens had an adult mentor at church who was not employed by the church.[7] Elsewhere he points out that for the next generation having relationships is essential. His logical conclusion is then that Churches need to help young people find personal mentors, and adults need to be those mentors.

Finally, in *Hurt 2.0*, Chap Clark takes a more passive role. His goal is simply explaining who 21st century teens are in their own words. He became part of the teens' world as their confidant. One off his key findings is that today's teens are the most relational generation ever – a finding some of the previous books mentioned but did not focus on. What matters to them is relationships, even over truth or moral issues (drinking for instance). Did you ever wonder why Facebook is such an obsession among teens?[8] He leaves it there but based on what he says, I think we can go a little further. Christ must be brought to this generation in a relationship. Mentoring is the most relational way to help teens – many other methods of youth ministry and catechesis are lacking precisely this key aspect.

Looking at studies showing how key personal faith is, we return to the previous Pew Research Center[9] study. Examining the factors for remaining Catholic, some elements surprisingly made no difference whatsoever: those who remained Catholics and those who left the Church went to catechesis and participated in Church-based youth activities at about the same rate. The biggest factor for remaining Catholic seems to be how strong their faith was as a teen. Those who stayed Catholic were twice as likely to report a strong faith as a teen. Faith is a personal relationship, not just an abstract belief. This is key for keeping the next generation of teenagers Catholic. Spiritual mentoring provides a personal relationship on a human level, giving the best environment for the supernatural relationship to develop.

Christian Smith concludes his book by describing teens' real religion as "moralistic therapeutic deism." For them, "God is a combination Divine Butler and Cosmic Therapist: he is always on call, takes care of any problems that arise, professionally helps his people to feel better about themselves, and does not become too personally involved in the process."[10] Their view of God is radically different from St Augustine's, who saw God as more intimate to him than he was to himself. [11] Mentoring gives them a personal view of God, a God who comes to them. It does this in two ways: directly, when we speak about God, and indirectly, when we come to them and care about them. One reason that their God is not involved in their lives is that so few adults are. Hopefully, they will go beyond just some God who is close to Jesus Christ. This is the God who is not only involved but saves. Mentoring is an ideal way to pass on the knowledge and experience of such a God.

Our main goal, however, is not to simply maintain the faith of those we direct but to help them grow so they can change this world for Christ, now and as adults. We want to disciple tens into apostles. St. Theresa of Lisieux is an example of what mentoring for an early age can do

God has created today's teenagers with a mission that they need to start now. Each generation has the responsibility to present the Gospel anew to its contemporaries in a language they can understand.[12] Many youth today no longer understand us. But if a few from their own generation speak, then they will understand the Gospel. We may only have the opportunity to help those few.

Since spiritual mentoring is personal, it tends to be deeper. If I know a teen deeply over a course of a few months or years, it's much easier for me to ask that they take the next step. This could be leading a mission to Haiti, taking on a leadership role in the group, doing 15 minutes of meditation every morning, or even committing their life to God in a vocation. The group can build up the general principles but individually can we reach much deeper. Many of the things listed could not be asked of a group; I can't ask everyone to enter the monastery. Even for those you can ask everyone like certain prayers, you need to ask them at different times to different people which can only be done in mentoring.

Society can only be changed one soul at a time. Spiritual mentoring connects his personality, his problems, and his life with Jesus. Regarding personal formation, John Paul II wrote:

To be able to discover the actual will of the Lord in our lives always involves the following: a receptive listening to the word of God and the Church, fervent and constant prayer, recourse to a wise and loving [mentor], and a faithful discernment of the gifts and talents given by God, as well as the diverse social and historic situations in which one lives.[13]

If we want to give teens a strong personal faith, if we want them to stay Catholic, if we want them to be active leaders in the Church, we must mentor them. Adults need to take interest in teens, lead teens in deep discussions, and help them become Christian adults – nothing can do this like mentoring. Mentoring can help teens see and accomplish God's wonderful plan for their life. No other means, no other method, can substitute this aspect of youth ministry. Despite all this evidence, this is the first book specifically dedicated to this type of mentoring.

2. WHERE DOES MENTORING FIT INTO COMPREHENSIVE YOUTH MINISTRY?

So that teens become the men that God is calling them to be, we need mentoring. However, for mentoring to be successful, certain elements are usually needed: some youth ministry, a mentor with specific qualities, and a high model to present to the teens we mentor.

Mentoring forms teens personally but will rarely work in a vacuum. A teenager lives among his friends. Teenage boys tend to get all nervous if you try to make appointments or make it too formal. If you need to provide all the virtues one-on-one, your mentoring session will go beyond the attention span of a teenage boy. For these reasons, mentoring should usually take place as part of a club, young group, scout troop, CYO team, or similar environment. It can also work in schools but only if those in charge are dedicated to the complete formation of the teens rather than just imparting a few intellectual lessons.

A second reason for working a youth ministry setting is that such a setting provides much of what the boy needs to become the man God calls him to be. It would be spiritual pride to think that we are the best in everything. Even if you are Mr. Perfect and break this mould, why are you running around like a chicken with your head cut off, rather than getting others take on those roles so these boys become apostles of Christ? Your special talent at mentoring will bear more fruit within a community: giving the teenager a positive environment and helping him become a complete Christian man is not the work of one, but of the whole faith community.[1]

Not only does the youth ministry environment help the boy prepare for mentoring, mentoring enriches the youth ministry environment. Since mentored teens should be growing more, they build up the youth ministry. Their growth should be returned to the group by taking on leadership roles.

In *Renewing the Vision*[2] (the guiding document on youth ministry from the US bishops) mentoring is an essential part of youth ministry. Mentoring is mentioned 6 times as part of youth ministry. It speaks of the need for adults who mentor teens, and of their need for mentors for their faith development. Beyond explicit mentions, 3 of the 8 components of comprehensive youth ministry – catechesis, leadership, and prayer – need mentoring to reach their maximum. Despite being listed as an important part, few youth ministries – besides those affiliated with Opus Dei and Regnum Christi – seem to have implemented it systematically.

Schools work very similar to youth ministry. The biggest difference is that the very fact it is *school* not *extra-curricular*, a certain degree of formality is expected. For example, I would never sit guys down in my office during youth ministry but I offer that option to the boys when doing it in a school. As well, if you do this at school, the administrators will probably expect you to focus a little more on study and assignments as resolutions – I find that works well. I have only just begun doing mentoring in a school a few months before publishing this so I think those working in schools can probably see how to adapt what I say regarding youth ministry to a school environment as good as I can.

Each mentor has certain natural qualities and difficulties

when approaching mentoring. When I first started out, I had to learn how to lower my explanations to their level, as I tended to be too intellectual. I remember trying to explain virtues straight from the Summa of St. Thomas Aquinas to a 7th grader without examples, and his eyes started to gloss over. Few of you are probably a nerd like I am, but none of us are perfect when we begin.

However, mentors need to have certain qualities. First of all for a boy, you need to be a *man*; woman are great leaders in the Church and do great with teenage girls, but the psychology of teenagers says that someone of the same gender will be a far better guide.[3] Teens are much more likely to open up to a non-parental adult of the same gender. I would not prohibit mentoring the opposite gender but I would seek to form mentors of both genders to help teens of their own gender. If only one person at a co-ed youth group is trained as a mentor, they usually need to be willing to take both genders to avoid parental complaints of favoritism. With multiple mentors (at least one of each gender), you will find the odd teen who will ask to speak with a mentor of the opposite gender. The main place I've seen this cross-over is teen girls wanting to deal with a priest.

The goal of mentoring is to help the boys become (1) virtuous (2) prayerful (3) Catholic (4) leaders. To be able to form the boys this way, a mentor needs to have all 4 characteristics; we are not asking for perfection but a real effort in all areas. If you aren't sure if you have one or the other, Appendix A brings these 4 attributes into daily life'. This Appendix offers a minimum baseline, but the words of St Bernard apply here: "He has ceased to be good whosoever does not desire to be better."[4] We need to grow in who we are so we can help teens grow in who they are.

As well, a mentor needs certain particular knowledge which this book will attempt to give. I attempt to explain mentoring in a practical manner – you could call this a "how-to" book – but without forgetting the principles so that you can adapt for the manifold situations each of you may be in. Become like

Christ to bring him to each boy.

We are not asking teens for a minimum, but instead, proposing a maximum ideal and helping the boys climb to that height. We want them to become Christian leaders that transform society. *101 Reasons to Wait for Marriage, Why Believe in Jesus,* and *Do I Have to Go to Mass?*⁵ can be good books for those youth who need them, but they can't be all that is offered, as so often is the case. Such minimalism presents three dangers: missing the opportunity to form saints, presenting the faith as a set of legal precepts, and failing to present the ideal of Christ. We all know many adult Catholics who could be so much if their Christian education when beyond minimalism.

If we do not form real leaders who dynamically live and transmit the faith, even in their youth, we will not have a positive and growing Church thirty years from now. The future of our Church depends on today's teens. Mentoring is a tool that can help in the Church's renewal. We must believe that God wants these boys to be saints; he wants everyone to be a saint. I recall a conversation I had with Steve who had been mentoring teens for four months.

"Mentoring is about forming the life of grace, right?" Steve asked.

"Yes. I personally prefer telling the boys 'friendship with Christ' but you can say 'the life of grace.'" I responded.

"Well, all the boys I see already live in the state of grace, so what do I do?" From a slight slip in vocabulary, I could see that he had also slipped into the minimalist view. Avoiding mortal sin (the state of grace) sufficed, so he didn't try to seek perfection (the life of grace) with the teens he saw. A long discussion ensued, in which I helped Steve see that a proper vision is beyond mere freedom for mortal sin.

In the Gospels we see that Jesus spent much of his time fighting minimalism. The Pharisees exemplify minimalism precisely because all of their laws were intended to fulfill the external aspects of what God wanted, a minimum. Instead of this attitude, "Jesus loved them to the end."⁶ He begins in the interior with love rather than in a legalistic, minimal fulfillment;

the Pharisees, despite seeming to be holy because they followed every nuance of the law, still only obeyed what they judged the minimum of the law. [7] This temptation reoccurs in every age. Christopher West expresses it thus:

> Fulfilling the law cannot be equated only with meeting the law's demands. It involves a super-abounding justice in man's heart and readily goes beyond the demands of the law out of a genuine love for truth. This is a "living morality" in which we realize the very meaning of being human. [8]

3. WHAT IS MENTORING?

Samuel called Trevor out of class for a regular session of mentoring. Before he could even begin, Trevor did:

"I can't stand Jacob; he is just driving me up the wall."

"How?"

"I just can't stand the way he laughs, the way he hogs all the attention. He never passes the ball in sports, and then he's always late so our team can never win anything. How am I supposed to put up with him?"

"Sure he isn't perfect but nothing you say says that he is really mean."

"Well, yah, I know"

"Well, our resolution last time was to work on charity, making two compliments to your friends a day,"

"Yes but what does that have to do with Jacob?"

"We agreed that Christ was the model of this charity, and where did he live his charity most dramatically?"

"I dunno, maybe with Mary as a boy."

"I think it was on the cross. Can you see him there? He is nailed to the cross, he was just whipped half to death, it's hard to breathe, he is quickly losing blood, the chief priests are mocking him, and his response is 'Father, forgive them.' This was not just words but forgiveness from the heart; he did not condemn them but forgave them. Following Christ's example, do you think you can forgive Jacob when he does things that annoy you?"

"Well, I'll try."

"We'll change the resolution a little for next time. Each day you can try to say one positive thing about Jacob to others or to him. Just focus on charity with him because if you can be charitable with him, you can be charitable with everybody else."

"OK."

Samuel then continued on with the other aspects of Trevor's life. This represents a fairly normal mentoring session: helping teens with prayer, virtue, and service to others.

Now, before we get into the meat, we need a starting definition of spiritual mentoring. Mentoring is a form of human communication but it is much more. It is a dialogue in faith. It doesn't go in circles but is for the betterment of the boy. The two of you together, in the Church and under the light of the Holy Spirit, seek God's will for him in the concrete circumstances of the life. A mentor is not a mere friend or a secular counselor, but commissioned by the Lord. Thus it is ecclesial according to St John of the cross.[1] Mentoring is similar to spiritual direction but it varies by several aspects we will now discuss'. After discussing the nature of mentoring in general, we will examine the characteristics proper to good mentoring, the art of listening, and Christ as the ideal mentor.

The General Nature of Mentoring

What is the nature of spiritual mentoring? Since spiritual mentoring and spiritual direction[2] are both forms of spiritual accompaniment,[3] let's begin with that. Spiritual accompaniment is a regular one-on-one dialogue with a person whom God puts on our path to lead us to himself (our true personal fulfillment as Christians);[4] this dialogue exists on the human level, but also on the supernatural level of faith.

As mentors, we are the ones put on the teens' path to grow closer to Christ. To be more fruitful, the relationship should be stable (one mentor per teen for an extended period). To grow, the teen must sincerely manifest his interior dispositions (i.e. his conscience) to you, and follow your advice with docility – so you better give him the right advice. We need to form their consciences, help them mature in their convictions, practice the virtues and follow Christ generously. Mentoring puts an immense weight on our shoulders.

Without question it is the soul who must walk this path, but it is the director's [or mentor's] responsibility to set forth the road to follow at each moment of his spiritual life. It is not a matter of pushing, but of softly guiding, respecting the freedom of souls.[5]

Before going on, we need to look at the two forms of spiritual accompaniment: mentoring and spiritual direction. The dividing line is not well defined, but instead, we have a gradual distinction between the two. Several times in this book I will refer to a teen progressing to spiritual direction which should be the natural process – a progression between the two. They are working towards the same goals and using similar methods. Mentoring is different form spiritual direction in that:

- Mentoring is not so exclusively focused on spiritual growth but covers a wider section of formation
- Mentoring is simpler and a beginning stage. Once souls advance it is inadequate
- In mentoring the mentor needs to take more initiative
  - o The mentor calls the boys while a directee usually calls his spiritual director to arrange an appointment.
  - o Usually during the session the mentor determines the themes, while usually the directee determines the themes in spiritual direction.
  - o Usually the directee in spiritual direction is expected to propose his own solution to a problem while younger teens in mentoring are often unable to do this yet.
  - o A directee should pick his spiritual director, while

often the adult leaders of a youth group can assign boys to mentors. (Such a list is obviously provisional because you need to be ready for boys who take to one mentor or another.)

- Mentoring is more casual, it is not an appointment with an expert but a chat with a friend and guide
  o In spiritual direction, "There is no strict obedience, [however,] there is what we may call an 'obedience' of prudence, following sensible and needed advice. In this ... meaning we 'obey' the directions of a medical doctor or a spiritual guide."[6] In spiritual mentoring, such obedience is advised but not even the obedience of prudence is insisted upon.
- Although confidential, mentoring doesn't have the same degree of confidentiality as spiritual direction. (Chapter 16 has a number of cases where you need to speak with the parents but a spiritual director would not share at all.)

In a way, spiritual mentoring is related to spiritual direction in an analogous manner to how other forms of mentoring and counseling are related to psychology. Both spiritual mentoring and counseling are a simplified versions which those without extensive professional training can do. My sister has a B.A. in psychology and is a social worker; she counsels people, but she can't do therapy because she lacks the training of a psychologist'. This analogy has one big caveat, usually people pass from counseling to psychological therapy because they are getting worse, while people pass from mentoring to spiritual direction because they are advancing.

We also need to distinguish spiritual mentoring from psychological mentoring. Most books on mentoring, basically teach simplified psychology. In many cases it would be recommended that Catholics do such mentoring, especially with troubled youth. Our goal cannot be psychological or the mere avoidance of evil; it is the spiritual, human, intellectual, and apostolic formation of the boy.

Mentoring can be explained by the four causes.[7] The material cause (that in which it has effect) is the soul of the boy directed. Even though you as a mentor are sanctified by mentoring and his body is affected by it, it is primarily focused on his soul. The formal cause (the change that occurs) is the specific guidance given following from his particular circumstances and the model Christ presents us. The agent cause (or who's causing the change) is primarily the Holy Spirit but we have to collaborate properly. For the final cause (the goal mentoring works towards), we go back to what Brian Bisgrove said. It is vocational as it is the means to discover what God wants the boy to do. This has three steps: First, it must vitalize their life by having them live spiritual life; second, grow in their love for Christ; and third, the boy needs to be active in both the youth group or club and in service projects or apostolates.[8]

Mentors must always remember that they form the most valuable creature in this universe: the human person. The goal is to form the boy into an apostle just like Michelangelo turned a rough rock in the Pieta. But since the boy is a person, he must become an active agent in his formation. It is hard for a boy to know and follow God's will. You, the mentor, must help him.

Every Christian needs to discover and follow God's will for their life. Mentoring helps boys do this so they can achieve personal fulfillment in God, with others, and through apostolate.

The growth of each will transform the Church and society. "Newman was of the view that the most important people in the Church are not the leaders but the teachers, and the latter due not so much to their writing as to their instruction."[9]

Before we go on, certain misconceptions need to be eliminated. Most were already addressed separating mentoring from spiritual direction and psychology but a few may still remain. Mentoring is not (1) a session of general spiritual advice, (2) a spiritual chat between friends in which no conclusion is reached, (3) a simple review of one's duties in life, (4) a tool to manipulate the boy to do your will, (5) a session on apostolate, or, finally, (6) a substitute dad. Even though training as a mentor will probably help you in your relationship with your son, don't confuse the roles.

Let's leave the definition for now since we will attempt a more complete one at the end of this first section. In general terms, spiritual mentoring is a regular one-on-one dialogue between you and a teenage boy with the goal of helping him grow humanly and spiritually to become the Christian that God is calling him to be. It is less formal and advanced than "spiritual direction."

Eight Qualities of a Good Mentoring Session

Following this general concept of mentoring, eight characteristics stand out as immediately relevant for every session. These will just be stated now. They will be developed throughout: some will be a point of discussion while others will lie behind several points.

Periodic: Just like any other type of growth, spiritual growth doesn't happen overnight. Holiness takes time. Mentoring is a concrete tool that, if applied with constancy, should help a boy grow spiritually. Keeping a set frequency is a must.

Motivating and demanding: The person being guided should leave a mentoring session very motivated and uplifted to keep fighting for sanctity. Boys need to be mentored in a positive environment, going back to the example Christ gives. Motivations vary from boy to boy and at times creativity is needed. We are indifferent if we don't demand from each soul – that is contrary to authentic love. Motivate in order to demand; never demand in order to motivate.

Profound: It should always be a deep dialogue of faith where the souls come face-to-face with Christ. Our long-term goal cannot be superficial – a resolution or fulfilling a norm – but deeper friendships with Christ.

Friendly: Mentors should imitate the merciful heart of Christ when dealing with souls. A mentor needs to be friendly without losing authority: boys often have trouble entrusting themselves to an authoritarian figure or someone artificially at their level. A good model for this is an uncle or older cousin whom they can confide in.

Concrete: Mentoring needs to be specific to help the boys. Mentors should always look to give specific examples and suggestions. Every session should end with a concrete resolution.

Sincere: On behalf of the person seeking to be mentored, sincerity is important. To be effective mentors must know the people they are guiding as well as possible. This should be clearly spelled out to teens the first time. Participants need to be transparent. They also need to be objective – neither too negative nor too optimistic regarding their spiritual life. Mentors have to help boys realize that to help them grow spiritually, they need to know the real person sitting before them and not the person he would like to be or hopes he will become. If you cough up blood then go to the doctor and talk about how you are beginning to bald, he will probably give you a prescription for Rogaine but you still have the same serious health issue. Mentoring is similar: without special inspiration from the Holy Spirit, your advice will be based upon what the teen said – if he hides something you can't be sure you sure giving him the right advice.

Faith: Absolute sincerity demands a good dose of faith. Teens need help to see that you, their mentor, are an instrument of the Holy Spirit. God really is present and blesses both you and him at that moment. Don't get proud, because God can speak and work through whomever he pleases when he wants to reach a soul.

Preparation: It helps if the boy thinks about mentoring beforehand, and this preparation should expand as he matures. You, on the other hand, *must* prepare. If boys know how to prepare for mentoring sessions should be deeper and more fruitful. The most important way to teach them this is by preparing yourself both in spirituality and in remembering the details of this particular soul.

The Art of Listening

Mentoring is a great opportunity to listen to the boy's soul. It is important for the mentor to realize this from the first moment, because he cannot guide souls if he does not know where those souls are. To know this, you need to listen.

Listening means letting the soul speak. It is a genuine interest in what he has to say because *he* says it, not just because of what he says; listening is intrinsically interpersonal. Boys will only be open if they know they are heard. Listening implies attention to the speaker but at times it also means clarifying, asking questions to fully understand or comprehend. Mentors need to do double listening because God wants to speak to them about the soul at the same time, and this requires faith.

One of sneakiest errors that can slip into mentoring is selective hearing; hearing only what you want to hear. This happens sometimes when one isn't attentive or is overly tired. If it happens frequently, it can indicate pre-judging the boys you are mentoring, where you no longer treat them as persons.

Christ the ideal Mentor

Christ is the ideal mentor. Every virtue that we want to practice in mentoring can be found in Christ. He unites and exemplifies all the characteristics just described. The Gospel has several examples of Christ as a mentor, but I want to focus on one here. You should take this to prayer.

Pick up your bible and read Luke 19:1-10 once through, and then have it beside you to see the exact passages as you read through this reflection. This needs to be a meditation where we aim to take on the characteristics of Christ in our mentoring. (Some other passages suggested for your own meditation on Christ as the ideal mentor are Luke 10:25-37; Luke 24:13-25; and John 21: 15-19.)

Zacchaeus was a man of low self-esteem, with no true friends, and generally hated because he was a tax collector. His encounter with Christ changed his life radically. Even before they met personally, something about Christ attracted him – he didn't believe too much in wonder workers, but this one was different. A mentor is one who is an example for the boys that they want to follow.

We all know he climbed a tree to see Jesus. St. Luke says that Christ "drew near" to him. Christ's "drawing near" expresses his capacity to put himself "in the other person's shoes," "drawing near" to the other person's feelings, thoughts and motivations. A mentor needs to "draw near" to the boy.

Christ called him, "Zacchaeus…" By calling his name, Jesus shows that he knows this man; with this little action he begins to stir the interior of this poor rejected man. Christ receives Zacchaeus. "Come down quickly, for today I must stay at your house." A mentor is positive and always motivating, always seeking opportunities to help the boy become more generous and a better friend of Christ.

Christ could have interrogated him about the seventh commandment or given evidence in front of everyone that Zacchaeus was a thief. But Jesus knew this was not the way to win that heart, and desired only to accompany him, without even bringing up the commandments. Responding to Christ's kindness, Zacchaeus himself changes from within. Hearing Christ's call, he left the sycamore and "received him with joy." During the meal, his soul continued its transformation, not so much because of what Christ said, but because of the way Christ treated him. Here we see the constancy that a mentor needs to have.

Christ teaches us mentoring, not by telling us, but by his actions. We can see how Christ applied the eight characteristics and how he listened. Mentoring was part of who he was. He saw it as a relationship to help others grow, ultimately leading them to the Father. However, at the same time, he didn't neglect the human aspect and came to people where they were.

4. WHO'S INVOLVED IN MENTORING?

Frank was praying. He had been mentoring Jonathan for a while. At first he grew a lot, but in the last few months, Jonathan didn't seem to be going anywhere; if anything he seemed to be going backward.

He felt the inspiration of the Holy Spirit that maybe he should mention purity. The next week he ran into Jonathan casually outside of an ordinary mentoring session. Nobody else would hear them, so he figured he would mention it:

"I hope that you are working well on your purity." Jonathan froze, then ran. For the next two weeks, every time Jonathan came into Frank's view, he quickly skirted away. Frank prayed for Jonathan. Every night he offered a special prayer for him. Then, Jonathan came up with a page that looked like he had ripped it out of his notebook and hid it in his pocket for a week. He handed it to Frank.

Frank opened the note and looked up quick enough to see a single tear fall and be wiped away. Then he read that Jonathan had masturbated. He folded the note and put his finger under Jonathan's chin to look him in the eye,

"I've never been so proud of you." Stunned, Jonathan

opened his eyes. "Because you did this," Frank continued "we can resolve your problem. The first step to rising up is admitting that you fell. And it is extra important because I know how embarrassed you are about this sin. If you are open, I can help you out."

"Really?" said Jonathan, letting out a breath of relief and revealing a small smile. Jonathan left this fall behind him and once again began his path towards holiness.

We say that *we* mentor teenage boys, but is that really what happens? The boys are not passive. And more importantly, neither we nor the teen are the center but rather the Holy Spirit. This story brings together the work of all three in mentoring.

We can easily think we do it all, but such an attitude sets you up for disaster. It seems that the Holy Spirit is at least a *little* more intelligent and powerful than we are. He is God, all-powerful, all-knowing, and all-good. As well, one of the greatest rewards of a mentor is when you can see a boy you have helped become a mature man who can make up his own mind. You don't want him to depend on you for simple things. When he is 16 or 18 he should be able to decide most things on his own and seek you out for the tough cases or to double-check. As mentors, we are in fact the least important of the three people present in mentoring.

We will address the Holy Spirit, then the mentor and finally the teen. I think this way will help show each one's role clearly.

The Holy Spirit

The Holy Spirit is the protagonist in mentoring. Our goal is the teen's growth and holiness. The mentor and the teen want it and work for it, but nobody wants it more than the Holy Spirit, and nobody can make it happen as he can.

> How do Christ and his Spirit act in the hearts of the faithful? Christ communicates his Spirit and the grace of God through the sacraments to all the members of the Church, who thus bear the fruits of the new life of the

Spirit. The Holy Spirit is also the master of prayer.[1]

Without the Holy Spirit nothing can be accomplished in the spiritual life – he is the Saint Maker. "Coming to live in our soul he transforms it into a *sacred temple* enriched with all manner of virtues."[2] He is the one who makes saints not us. He is the potter; we are the clay that becomes the work of his hands.[3]

The Holy Spirit has a plan for each mentor and each boy: "The vision is unique to your circumstances and calibrated to your abilities. Why would he bother? Because God is your partner in ministry."[4] Holiness is the happy result of a divine partnership, a joint venture. It is obviously an unequal partnership. God chooses to work with and through us, we have not chosen him.[5] Through brief mentoring sessions, the transcendent goal is to have each soul discover the divine partnership and begin his own sanctification.

As Jesus promised at the last supper, he sends us the Holy Spirit to "teach us all things… and guide [us] into truth."[6] We need open our ears, eyes, minds, and hearts. He urges us on. He consoles. He strengthens.

Be attentive to his inspirations: once they are heard, don't delay. Obey. In mentoring this is key because it is a special time of God's grace where both the boy and mentor should be extra attentive: often God's grace only comes once. Pope Benedict said: "It is only when a young man has a personal experience of Christ that he can truly understand the Lord's will and consequently his own vocation."[7]

A consequence of this is the importance of our prayer. We should never begin a mentoring session without at least some brief prayer. We should regularly pray for the teens we mentor. Our intercessory prayer lets God touch them and transform them in ways we can't. I'll develop this in Chapter 16.

The Mentor

The mentor is you! You are called to lead another soul towards holiness, cooperating with the grace of the Holy Spirit and using the means recommended by the Church. You are called, for a brief or extended period of time, to be a special instrument of spiritual and personal growth for a teen.

Although it is true that a mentor is primarily God's instrument, he needs to form himself in certain virtues. He is not a paintbrush in an artist's hand but an active participant who contributes with his intellect, will and body. Mentors need to acquire a wide range of virtues. Francis de Sales emphasizes three qualities: "He must be full of charity, knowledge, and prudence, if he lacks one of these there is danger."[8] These qualities are expressed in the following virtues which can all be acquired:

- Knowledge of **Catholic doctrine and spirituality:** we mentor according to true catholic spirituality.
- **Balance and realism:** boys tend to exaggerate things and need a mentor who is solid and realistic to draw them out of occasional dreams. To this end, basic psychology is helpful; but he must avoid the tendency to psychologize everything or reduce everything to one cause.
- **Personal strength:** A mentor must guide and not be guided by the boys.
- **Inspiration:** A mentor needs to always be a motivating example for the teens.
- **Clarity:** A mentor needs to communicate very clearly.
- **Faith in Christ:** if Christ and his desires are not strongly rooted, a mentor will not be able direct souls towards the greatest good. He should pray for God's light.
- **Trust:** Mentoring is first of all a relationship of trust. An open and merciful heart, adapting to each soul, humility in accepting and following others' judgments, avoiding favoritism among the boys directed, and down to earth advice gain boys' trust. On the other side, a mentor needs to believe in the boy he directs; believe that this boy can do something amazing for Christ.
- **Reserve:** A mentor needs to maintain the confidences received in mentoring. Boys need assurance that nothing

they say will leave the silence of their mentor's heart.[9] (Later, specific exceptions such as serious sin and abuse will be elaborated.)

- **Charity:** A mentor always has a heart for helping each boy become the best he can be. This is expressed in his concern in mentoring but cannot be limited to that. Charity is a way of life.

The Teenager

The goal of mentoring is the teen's transformation. Therefore, we need to know teenagers. Teenage boys are unique human beings created in God's image and likeness, baptized Catholics, adolescents who are discovering themselves, and meaning-seekers.[10] Keep each aspect in mind. Participants should also be seeking mentoring so as to be able to grow in their friendship with Christ.

To make good use of mentoring, teenage boys need to approach it with 4 attitudes:

Supernatural: Mentors only seek souls' spiritual good. Boys need to realize that. Mentoring draws the boy to a deeper relationship with Christ and a better fulfillment of his commitments as a Christian and those he has freely assumed by joining a Catholic youth group.

Sincere and open: If a boy doesn't open himself sincerely to his mentor, it's rather useless. Mentoring should give his life direction but to use a map, you need to know where you are. Most mentors can't intuit via ESP. The mentor needs to be dedicated and trustworthy for a teenage boy to open up.

Docile: 99% of the growth in spiritual life happens outside of mentoring. During mentoring, a map is drawn, but participants need to walk the path when they leave. If a teen doesn't try to grow outside of mentoring, he's like a man wanting to climb a mountain who asks a guide for help, but never follows the guide's instructions. Often boys fail to act because they fail to see the larger vision and the ultimate goal which need to be explained clearly.

Discreet: This is important for the mentor to explain that everything remains between them and God (rare exceptions later). Also, it is important for teens to be discreet about what they say, with regards to the advice received from their mentor – because it has to do with a personal relationship with Christ. Perhaps the advice given to one person is not the best advice to be given to another. For example one could have the resolution to be less overbearing while the other has the resolution to be more assertive.

5. WHERE DOES MENTORING COME FROM?

Back about 1600 years ago, a man named Paphnutius (imagine having that name) had been out in the desert 21 days (with only 4 days of food) looking for some holy monks. He saw a man in the distance, covered in hair more than his raged clothes. Paphnutius ran in fear to a nearby cliff and tried to hide himself amidst the plants. A voice thundered:

"Come down from the mountainside, you man of God. Don't be afraid. I am just a frail mortal man like you." Realizing that this must be one of the holy monks he was looking for, he scrambled down and knelt down before him.

"Get up, get up," he said. "You mustn't kneel before me. You too are a servant of God and your name is Paphnutius, beloved of the Saints." Surprised that the man knew his name, he got up with joy.

"God who has guided me through the desert has fulfilled my heart's desire," said Paphnutius. "My limbs and joints which were almost disintegrating begin to feel refreshed. But my mind still thirsts for enlightenment. Tell me, reverend sir, with a fervent heart I beg you, I appeal to you in the name of him for the sake of whose love you inhabit the lonely wastes of this desert, whence did you come? What is your name? How long have you been here? I beg you, tell me plainly."

"I can see," the man replied, "how earnestly you wish to know about the tribulations of my long life, beloved brother. Have no fear, I shall tell you everything, right from the beginning. I am called Onuphrius, an unworthy sinner, and I have been living my laborious life in this desert for nearly seventy years. I have the wild beasts for company, my regular food is fruit and herbs, I lay my miserable body down to sleep in mountainsides, in caves, and in valleys. Throughout all these years I have seen no one except you, and I have not been supplied with food by any human being." And they continued talking for a long while so Paphnutius could also become a holy monk.[1] They are both honored as saints.

You will probably have very few mentoring sessions like that. This is one of the first stories we have of something akin to mentoring. Despite how far it is from our experience, some elements of mentoring are already present: it is a one-on-one dialogue, it is personal (he called his name), it is under the light of the Holy Spirit, guidance is sought, and the relationship is directed towards the formation of Paphnutius.

Mentoring may seem like a new concept to some. It isn't; instead, it comes from a long tradition in the Church in a manner adapted to our day. Speaking one-on-one about one's personal and spiritual life comes to us from Biblical traditions, and from the tradition in the Church. Mentoring is related to all personal formation but it comes specifically from the stream of spiritual direction. This is an ancient practice in the history of salvation and the early Church which has developed through a series of saints to what we have today.

We see that God comes to man personally in the Bible. At the starting point of human history, God walked with Adam and Eve as a friend;[2] Moses had the experience of talking with God "face to face."[3] St. Joseph received his divine instructions in dreams.[4] If someone searched Sacred Scripture for a foundation for mentoring, they would find many exhortations to follow the counsel of a prudent man. Samuel learned to hear

God through the prophesies of Eli; Cornelius was sent to St. Peter by God; the scales did not fall from St. Paul's eyes until he talked with Ananias, and on other occasions *he* consulted St. Peter. [5]

Christ is both teacher and Son: from these titles, the Church has developed various types of relationships for one-on-one direction. In the early Church, the teacher-disciple relationship flourished. It was a relationship in which the master transmitted ideas, thoughts, and concepts, not only through words, but also through his example and accompaniment. Considered masters of life, these mentors transmitted not only theoretical concepts, but also instruction in all aspects of life and morality. The apostles were sent forth to preach, baptize, and transmit all that Jesus said and did, and in so doing, they carried out their mission as true "spiritual fathers." When new Christian communities were founded, the apostles were careful to leave worthy men in authority to direct the community, which would include some personal attention akin to mentoring.

In monastic life, the abbot took on the relationship of spiritual fatherhood. As the holiness of the hermits and monks became known, people began to seek them out for advice and counsel. As communities were formed, the practice of personally speaking to the abbot of the monastery, or to another experienced monk, became institutionalized in these monastic communities. This form of spiritual accompaniment became an ordinary practice. This "spiritual direction" that took shape in monastic times continued throughout the Middle Ages. In the twelfth century, St. Francis of Assisi and St. Dominic intensely recommended this practice in order to achieve spiritual perfection.

The Renaissance marks the beginning of the modern era, a time full of challenging circumstances for the Church. Great saints, such as St. Ignatius of Loyola, St. Francis Xavier, St. Teresa of Avila, St. John of the Cross, St. Francis de Sales, St. Philip Neri, and St. Vincent de Paul, were all on the front lines of Catholic renewal and recommend one-on-one direction.

Spiritual direction which had begun with monks, moved slowly to include a wider breadth of people: bishops, priests, and eventually laity of diverse ages (physically and spiritually).

Throughout the centuries, the Church relied on the experience of its "pioneers" in the spiritual life. Today, faithful Catholics who write and teach about the spiritual life, or ascetic and mystical theology, embrace the Church's teaching and continue to recommend spiritual direction or mentoring. This practice encompasses the forms we have discussed: the master-disciple and spiritual father-child relationships, consultation with someone learned and holy, and personal, regular spiritual formation. John Paul II wrote:

> To be able to discover the actual will of the Lord in our lives always involves the following: a receptive listening to the Word of God and the Church, fervent and constant prayer, *recourse to a wise and loving guide*, and a faithful discernment of the gifts and talents given by God, as well as the diverse social and historic situations in which one lives.[6]

As spiritual direction became more common, it took on several formal elements. Some of these formal elements are inappropriate for teenagers, so they will not be included in mentoring. Spiritual mentoring is a more basic type of direction than spiritual direction even though it draws a lot of inspiration from it. It's not something new, but springs from practices recommended for all Catholics. It will not be available to every Catholic teen today. Hopefully, through those of you reading this book, it will become available to a few more.

Definition of a Mentor

Before we conclude this first section on mentoring in general, we need to try to give a definition of a mentor based on all we have seen. Let's lay out the necessary elements. First, a mentor is one who accompanies teens one-on-one but is associated with some Catholic youth ministry, so he must collaborate with the other leaders. Because it is one-on-one, all he offers is personalized. Second, a mentor is one who the boys look up to, someone they strive to be like; thus a mentor must always treat them positively and be an example. Third, his first concern is each boy's holiness and Christian formation; he helps the teen grow humanly and spiritually to become the Christian that God is calling him to be.

With these elements, we can give an approximate definition of mentoring. Mentor: a dynamic, prayerful, Catholic man who accompanies teenage boys one-on-one within youth ministry to help them with their overall formation, but especially with their personal holiness in a personal and positive environment. It probably isn't perfect; but it at least gets the essentials. As you read each chapter in this book, different aspects should be understood more profoundly, and then when you finish, you can come back to this definition as a summary.

We are now going to make a huge loop before getting to practical suggestions on mentoring in the last section. We first need to understand *who* the teen is in a way that we can form him with an adequate pedagogy. Then we need to understand *where* we are going with a section on spiritual growth adapted to teenage boys.

THE ADOLESCENT: PEDAGOGY THAT ENTERS HIS WORLD

This section explains who the teen is and how we form him. It begins with the basic philosophy and philosophy of man. Then it moves to the stages of being a teenager and the parts of teen life. Then it moves on to pedagogy: areas of formation, principles, and your role as a mentor in this whole matrix.

6. TEENS ARE PERSONS

When one of my sisters recently got married, they made an album of selected photos of the bride and groom. One stood out to me by the way it described us four Schneider kids. At first glance there's just four kids aged 1 to 11 sitting on a couch. The difference came analyzing the four.

I sit in the middle with my "Dinosaur Country Science Camp" t-shirt on, immersed deep in thought. On one side one sister has her arms stretched straight up and an excited look on her face. On the other side, another sister gently holds the baby who seems to enjoying being caressed by her older sister. From this one snapshot, you can see our four personalities. You probably even know which one is the social worker I mentioned earlier.[1]

When you mentor a boy, who do you see? Jason Taylor? One more boy you have to mentor? An adolescent who can change this world for Christ? *Who* we see affects *how* we direct the boy. Each boy is different just like each of the Schneider kids but all have certain similar aspects.

To be able to help him, you need to see all the aspects of who he is. Otherwise, you will be unable to realistically help. In this section we deal with what it means to be a person and try to give a quick overview of the psychological, physiological, and spiritual changes normal for teens. Despite being based in large part on psychology and philosophy, we transcend this base in our focus on spiritual growth. Mentoring should form the man, the saint, and the apostle. This section focuses on the formation of the man – the Christian man – who happens to be a teenager.

In this chapter, we will try to grasp *who* this teen is. We are going to get a little philosophical and some of you may need to read this twice to understand (I had to read the book three times when I learned this stuff). We begin by talking about the person as a whole, then move to the various faculties, and we conclude by bringing this all into a pedagogical perspective.

Who Is the Human Person Standing Before Me?

The starting point is the definition of "person." In the last few centuries, a myriad of definitions of person: if this were a philosophy course, it might be interesting to review them all'. We will focus, however, on the classical definition. A human person is a spiritual (thinking) animal – the bridge between two worlds – material (what can be seen, touched, grasped, etc.) and the spiritual (what cannot be seen, but is more real). In recent years, some have proposed "incarnate spirit" instead of "spiritual animal": I think in the end it basically means the same thing, but approaches it from the spiritual and invisible side, rather than the material and tangible.

We are our flesh and bones, but we are not *just* our flesh and bones; we have a spiritual soul that sets us apart from everything else in this world. I am a *who*, not a *what*. A material creature (a dog for example) can be trained with pure rewards and punishments, but a human being can transcend his instincts. No dog has ever gone on a hunger strike over cruelty to animals. Persons can make free decisions out of love which is not feeling but self-giving to another.

However, God goes beyond our basic definition: "Then God said, 'Let us make man in our *image*, after our *likeness*.'"[2]

This is how God sees each boy. We are created in his image and likeness, wounded by sin, and redeemed by Jesus Christ.

Because we created in God's image and likeness, we are able to love. Whence comes our dignity as human persons – we are sons of God, created by him, to be like him. When it's difficult to deal with a certain boy, find the divine image in him! It *is* there. "Human beings are more than the sum of the good they accomplish. They are children of God."[3] Before anything a boy does, remember who he is.

Sometimes it is hard to find that image because every person has a wounded tendency towards sin. As a mentor, you may often find the soul walking with you who views his life through the perspective of his own selfishness, not wanting to be honest with God, or struggling to fulfill the simplest of commitments.

Though each person possesses weaknesses, it is all the more important to remember the last part of the theological definition – each person is redeemed by Christ. He shed his blood to show the way to the Father. He shows human beings how to walk the path to life seeking heaven. It is this search for friendship with Christ and holiness that is the basis for mentoring. Remember, everything is possible with God and you need to keep this in mind when working with the boy before you. He has redeemed mankind and conquered sin. He has opened the gates of heaven for every individual. The friendship we have with him on earth continues in heaven.

We understand teens as human persons; this means they exist in both the physical and the spiritual. Moreover, they are children of God called to a relationship with him.

Faculties of the Human Person

"Faculties" may sound abstract but a faculty is simply the capacity to do something that comes naturally, rather than with training. We have faculties to eat, to sleep, to speak, to reason, etc.[4] 'As already mentioned, the human person has this mystery of two worlds within them: the union of the body and soul.

Therefore, different faculties exist in body and soul. A bland comparison could be a hunting rifle: one part of it is designed for firing a bullet that will take down a game animal, and the other part of it is designed to protect you by holding it firmly against your shoulder. This second part is inferior, serving the first part. Likewise, the bodily faculties should serve the spiritual ones. Because of the existence of both body and soul – not just one or the other – humans are capable of doing certain acts. This sets us apart. Like with the definition of the person, I have preferred the traditional view over the myriad of modern options – I think it expresses these faculties better.

The bodily faculties make persons similar to animals. They are the exterior and interior senses, appetites, instincts, and locomotive ability'. We focus on these to the extent they play upon and affect the spiritual faculties; this particularly concerns the internal faculties like memory, imagination, and appetite.

These bodily faculties have natural tendencies toward certain things. Based on their duration and intensity, we can divide them into sentiments, moods, passions and motivations.

1) **A Sentiment:** It is a psychological phenomenon – an emotion if you prefer that word – which is subjective and has diverse causes, favorable or unfavorable. It comes and goes like the wind. As a mentor, you need to help boys know these sentiments will come and go always; even the change of weather can cause them, so they do not need to give them much importance.

2) **A Mood:** It is more conscious than a sentiment and has a longer duration. It does not just come and go. They are caused by the same "variable" factors that cause sentiments, but they are lasting – either because they are fostered in the heart or the circumstances are general or long-term. Sentiments and moods should not be the guiding light for life. They need to be controlled or they will blow man from one pole to the other. Faith, intelligence, and willpower need to direct sentiments and emotions towards truth and action in accordance with the greater good.

3) **A Passion:** Intensity distinguishes a passion: it's a very strong feeling or overwhelming emotion. In a positive way, passions point to Christ's passion and death. He had a great love for souls which moved him to the ultimate sacrifice. Examples of negative passions are anger, jealousy, or greed. When strong negative feelings get out of control, they lead to negative actions.

4) **A Motivation:** Beyond a mere "sentimental" level, a motivation is a deep affection that leads to a consistent mode of acting. They present the will with a good to be obtained. This is a long term goal or attitude which drives the will: like a group of 7th graders who want to win the state football championship in High School.

Spiritual faculties, as opposed to bodily ones, are those which make persons thinking beings, reflections of God. These spiritual faculties are intelligence and will. This course focuses more on getting to know these superior faculties or capabilities of the human person, since they are what makes one more like God and helps direct the bodily faculties, thus moving along the path to sanctity.

Intelligence is not a reference to being smart. It is where we capture the reality of an object on a spiritual level; where we understand; where we know truth. A classic definition is "the capacity to grasp the *being* of things." As a mentor, you need to help form the boy beyond mere feelings so he sees the truth and the deeper meaning clearly – to analyze their lives, to learn to relate experiences, to form right judgments of situations and people.

It is the one faculty human persons have that is not "blind". It is led by and seeks the truth. It is also enlightened by the light of faith. As a mentor, it is important to realize intelligence is the faculty where convictions reside. It adheres to truth. If you want to help a boy build strong convictions in his friendship with Christ, his faith and in his life, you need to help him discover and adhere to truth in such a way that he never doubts.

Through man's everyday choices, he determines his

fundamental option, the overall direction of his life. This happens in the will. The will is the capacity to desire and to choose with freedom; and such choices determine us as persons. As we received the reality outside ourselves with our intellect, we direct ourselves to the outside reality with our will; it responds to what we have received in the intellect illuminated by faith. It is the capacity to choose the true good. Sometimes, however, one can mistake certain things for "good", when they are really harmful. To form the will, you must remember it is a "blind" faculty: it will only go for the good that the intelligence presents.

When motivating a boy to do something or strengthen his willpower, he needs to understand why the right choice is good. This understanding helps him act now and in the future. Laziness can seep in during this period in their life, and forming the will counteracts this. It is in the will that love is found, for love consists in: "that the lover wills the good for his loved one."[5] Only this faculty loves. One who loves not only does his duty but goes beyond it. Love is the driving force of man.

Thus we see how man has both bodily and spiritual faculties which give him the capability to achieve a wide range of different acts. The bodily faculties are very important but they need to be submitted to the illumination of the intelligence and guided by love.

A Pedagogical View of the Human Person

Caleb was always a little antsy at camp. His red hair stood out wherever trouble was brewing. Some might have thought of him as a trouble-maker, but his mentor saw a well-intentioned 11 year-old who was just a little fun-loving. Slowly but steadily he helped him grow virtue by virtue. He gave him greater and greater responsibilities: leading a squad, directing an event, etc. By 16, Caleb would wake up half an hour before the other campers to do his own meditation in the chapel before waking them up. Caleb is a perfect example of a pedagogical approach.

From the perspective of our faith, we know that God has a plan for each teenage boy. Pedagogy is what helps us see what that is concretely for this boy rather than just in general as we have seen with the person and the faculties. A Christian pedagogy is based on one model – Jesus Christ – and the manifold ways teens are called to imitate him.

Christ is the model. Man – as a philosophical concept and in everyday life – is a mystery, and "it is only in the mystery of the Word made flesh that the mystery of man truly becomes clear"[6] To form a boy, we must start on the supernatural plane with such a model. The model of Christ is supernatural, but he presents us a complete person replete with all the virtues. John Paul II wrote: "The decisive answer to every one of man's questions … is Jesus Christ himself."[7]

To form a boy we need a vision of man that is down to earth but at the same time not limited to earth – a realistic anthropology. When we begin with the Gospel, we see man and the world full of love, respect, admiration, and hope. Man has these values within himself; however, many things in this valley of tears distract him from his divine vocation. This perspective helps us form teens as humans and Christians.

As mentors, above all else you are trying to help the boys be more like Christ, be his friend, and fulfill their Christian vocation. We must set our sights high. Realism is not wallowing in the bare minimum but seeing the vision that God has for each boy and helping him achieve that vision. Mentoring boys, we cannot forget this vision.

Each teenager we work with is a human person created in God's image. He has faculties to direct his life by. However, in the end, these all converge on Jesus, who is the ideal each teen strives towards. If we view teens this way, we give them the opportunity to become saints. And Benedict XVI told youth: "The saints, as we said, are the true reformers. Now I want to express this in an even more radical way: only from the saints, only from God does true revolution come, the definitive way to change the world."[8]

7. ADOLESCENT PSYCHOLOGY

"OK," I begin with this group of high school guys, "do you have a soul? But before you answer, we have one rule, no using the bible or the catechism till the end."

"Well, yah…" says one boy across the dining room table.

"But why? Can you prove it to me?" Silence reigns over the group. I prod again,

"What does it mean to have a soul? Would you all agree that it means that there is some part of us that isn't material?" Their heads nod. "So what are some properties that all material things have?" Now they start responding with intelligent answers. This is the beginning of an activity I have run successfully several times with high school young men. It shows one aspect of the formation we can offer teens, and the fact I have never done this with 6th-graders shows adolescent development.

We are forming teenage boys: they are no longer children but not yet permitted to enter the adult world. "Adolescence is not a blend of both child and adult, nor is it an expanded phase of either. Adolescence is a unique phase of life that must be understood and dealt with on its own merits."[1] We need to understand them, not just human beings in general, not just the spiritual life, not just one one-on-one dialogue. We each have our own experience of the teenage years which helps us understand what they are going through, but it would be a pity if we remain with our subjective experience.

This chapter is intimately linked with the following. Here we speak about the psychological growth of the boy, there we will speak of the formation that corresponds to this growth. These two chapters could be a book in themselves and it may seem like we are flying through. Don't worry if you don't understand this all now; you can come back to this chapter after you are done with the book.

Between 11 and 18, teens change from being mere boys to being men. They may seem all over the place, but this is only because of the growth that's happening. Below this age, mentoring (except by a dad) would do little, and it suffices to treat them as a group. By 16 to 19, a boy should be ready for full spiritual direction, which should is a transition from mentoring that focuses more exclusively on the spiritual aspect and is for discerning God's will, not simply forming oneself to be ready to discern.

This material will also be helpful when we speak of a teenage spirituality as it corresponds to this growth. In this chapter, we will explore adolescent development by looking at the stages, a boy's relationships with others, and his spirituality. We will leave the other aspects to the summary given in Appendix B.

Stages of Adolescent Development

The physiological, psychological, and spiritual changes a person experiences during the teenage years can define the person's course in life. Before we speak of stages, we need to understand adolescence as an "independent search for a unique identity or separateness, with the end goals being a certain knowledge of who one is in relation to others, a willingness to take responsibility for who one is becoming, and a fulfilled commitment to live with others in community."[2] To accompany boys at this age, we need to understand their particular strengths and weaknesses.

What I give is a general rule; genetics and other factors can put boys a year ahead or behind, so don't apply this too squarely. Until 11 or 12, they are still children with little physiological differentiation from girls; after this follows three stages of adolescence.

Puberty: (12 to 14 in boys) Physical changes begin in boys and affect their psychology. Hormonal changes tend to make them tired. Interiorly, they want to begin defining themselves: they change how they act and want to attempt this self-definition.

Middle Adolescence: (14 to 16 or 18 in boys) This is the moment of identity crisis. They begin to ask existential questions: Who am I? Why does the world exist? Evidently, this leaves a certain instability and insecurity; they would like to be adults but without the responsibility that is necessary. Their mind and heart have not caught up to the body, yet.

Late adolescence: (about 17 to individuation in young men) They begin settling down, knowing and accepting themselves and the world around them. This often ends quickly, but today can drag on into the mid-20s. The end goal of this period is not physiological or emotional. When he is psychologically and socially independent, he defines himself and takes responsibility for who he is and who he's becoming. [3]

As the teens progress through these stages, it is not just one aspect of their life that changes but a multitude of interrelated dimensions. Most books focus on the physiological and emotional dimensions – thus they are well known and I will only mention them. Our focus will instead be on the interpersonal and spiritual dimensions, which are key for mentoring but less well known.

Puberty is all of the physical development that comes with sexual maturity: this is not limited to the physical aspects but affects the affections, the psyche, all the way down to our intellect and will – man's true heart. Their hormonal changes should lead to personal development. It is a time with intensified emotions that are often on a roller coaster, especially in middle adolescence. They can rebel, but this self-affirmation and self-definition can be directed positively; in fact, rebellion is often an attempt to affirm they are adults, and such boys usually mature if given adult responsibilities.[4] At 11 girls still have cooties, but by 16 they are an attractive other who draws forth an emotional response from the young man.

Because they are on an emotional rollercoaster, the danger of basing their personal development on emotions rather than convictions is multiplied.[5] Emotions are only part of the picture; they should not be the basis of convictions or guidelines for decisions. It should not matter how something feels – but rather is it right? Is it good? At times they need help keeping their feet on the ground between wild emotions and crazy dreams.

Friends and Family

Every teenager should grow immensely in his interpersonal skills. Because he now defines himself, he becomes truly sociable. He now tends towards his friends but still is rooted in his family. Among his friends, often a certain girl will become his girlfriend. These varied environments contribute to his development. Here we will explore friends, girlfriends and then family, but first one warning about extremes.

In their development of their ethical attitude towards society, they can have extreme views of the world. It can be a pessimistic view of the world where everything seems to be going wrong; an optimistic view, wanting to change the world and feeling they will be the world's super hero; or a judgmental view where even the smallest decision becomes absolute ("he's going to hell because he smokes"). Mentors should help them get a balanced view and see how much Christ can do. They want to put their big ideals into action. Help channel these efforts towards something concrete and good via mentoring. They also need to learn how to relate with others outside of their group, especially accepting others who are different.

Now, they are conscious of themselves, their own life and their position in the world, but lack experience: help them learn to relate with others. They needs to feel accepted by others to accept themselves – thus friendship development is key. (Compare how many have kept up with their high school friends at 40 and how many have kept up with their elementary school friends.) Since they feel insecure in this world, they will often defend themselves against the world of adults. Their group of friends is the center of their life, but help them avoid forming a cliquey attitude which cuts them off from the outside world.

A teen's primary social atmosphere is his friends. We need to know both who his friends are and what they do so we can help the whole group. At school he not only has his friends, but the stress from tests and grades which grow exponentially during these years. Despite the influence of the school, the primary influence group is his friendship group.

Mass media also has a great influence. Television, YouTube, movie theatres, Wii, online games, facebook, blogs, , iPhones, twitter, music, Google, etc. are all elements in the social environment that influence and make up this world of the adolescent. In 2010, an average teen consumed almost 8 hours (7:39) of media on an average day.[6] This can lower moral standards if it involves, as it often does, repeating immoral images and sounds which are made normal by such repetition.

As we move towards older boys, the whole question of a girlfriend will become an important facet of their life; at this stage in their life, however, it should not become their whole life. Generally, group activities with both guys and girls are to be preferred. When pairing off happens too quickly it destroys the opportunity to build a relationship of friendship first, it cuts off other relationships, it tends towards intimacy before commitment, and it takes the boy's focus away from forming himself for the future. *Chastity is not a line but a direction.* [7] We must encourage boys to make the positive steps in this direction as only then will then be ready to make a self-gift when it is called for: "Only when a person is liberated from lust and is in possession of his own sexual subjectivity can he be a gift for others."[8]

In sexual intimacy one speaks with one's body. We generally think of this focusing on the marital act, but it is true with much lesser forms of intimacy like kisses and caresses. The sexual act is the culmination of a loving relationship, not a pure mechanical act. Once a man loves a woman fully in all the other ways, he completes his love with sex. Having sex before committing to marriage is like eating a jar of maraschino cherries and not enjoying an ice cream sundae. Sure the cherry is a highlight of a sundae but eating them by the jar is not nearly as nice. Great sex must be preceded by a great relationship.

In effect, the marital act says "I love you so much that I need more to love since you alone are cannot contain all the love I have for you." It is, after the sacraments, the deepest interpersonal relationship available on earth. This is one reason why marriage is sometimes called the primordial sacrament. This is why sex must always be both unitive and procreative. Either without the other lacks such an interpersonal relationship of love.

Other acts of intimacy are also forms of deep interpersonal relationships. By romantic kissing, the two enter a kind of intimacy and communion of love. If this intimacy is built upon truth it is much more satisfying. If instead, that intimacy is based solely on a mutual agreement to derive pleasure from the other, it will not satisfy the longings of the teen's heart. In fact such false intimacy adds calluses to the heart which are hard to remove when he wants true intimacy.

The difference between true and false here is sometimes hard to determine from the outside. But in mentoring we can see the teen from inside where the difference is obvious – what is the goal of this intimacy? Intimacy directed towards a possible marriage (and thus for the other) is different than intimacy for one's own enjoyment. Sometimes love is defined as willing the good of the other before one's own good. This definition helps us see if the intimacy the boy is engaging in is true love or not.

Jesus goes so far as to say, "Everyone who looks at a woman lustfully has already committed adultery with her in his heart."[9] Obviously this would not include every lustful thought because often they are beyond our control. Some teens will get scrupulous and we need to explain that when the thoughts are beyond our control they are not sinful. For example, no sin is involved in having a sexual thought while passing the magazines in the checkout line but grabbing one to search out similar images inside would often count as one. In Theology of the Body, John Paul II clarifies that this adultery in the heart happens when the other is no longer seen as a person, as an "other" but is reduced to an object of our pleasure. In this way it is not just that a boy sees a Bikini-clad woman but how he looks at that woman. This distinction can be seen in the difference of a naked woman in classical art and in pornography – in art she is shown with respect and as a beautiful person, in pornography she is an object meant to arouse.

Long-term exclusive dating (not asking a different girl out each weekend of going out on "group dates") when marriage is not a realistic possibility on the horizon seems to make little sense. The more important principle is a purity of heart which treats girls with respect and sees exclusive dating as a preparation for marriage. A boy who is set to take over his dad's farm will probably be ready for marriage a whole lot sooner than one whose plans include an Ivy League law degree; hence he will be ready for exclusive girlfriends much earlier.

Personally, I only had one girlfriend. A little after our amicable breakup I read *I Kissed Dating Goodbye* by Joshua Harris and decided that I was going to wait until halfway through college before going out again – and God called me to the religious life just before halfway. In retrospect that choice was much more mature than most of my peers' choices. Why such a choice? For me it was very simple, until I was able to support a kid I wasn't ready for marriage, going out with a girl when that was more than 2-3 years out was not fair to her or my emotions, and I wanted a job that required a University degree. I liked girls and there were a handful I would have definitely gone out with had I not made that commitment.

As far as I can see, the primary goal of exclusive dating is to find a spouse. If marriage is not in the picture or so far off, a teen should ask himself if the relationship is in the *direction* of chastity, and if there are other things God may be asking him to do with his time now. However, I don't think that we should force rules on teens beyond respect for whatever rules their parents have. In fact given the diverse life-goals, situations, and personalities of teens, I would hesitate even to give any specific rules. Instead, as mentors we need to present a global vision and the beauty of sex, marriage, and the rest of Christian life so teens freely choose chastity. If instead of choosing to wait on my own some authority had forced not dating upon me, I probably would have found a way to date.

We want to train teens to be rebels against the cohabitation generation. Romance, sex, and babies no longer have anything to do with marriage. About 2/3 of my classmates from elementary school are currently living-with instead of living-for (i.e. married to) another. Marrying is already counter-cultural, how much more counter-cultural they will be if that is their concrete goal from their teen years. We mentors need to strengthen teens so they can make these decisions but we can't make their decisions for them.

The culture attacks this area relentlessly, pounding sexual messages into boys' heads. Many boys who want to follow Christ will try to see how close to the "chastity line" they can get without sinning. Even if they don't cross it, this method fails because it reduces love to law. Moreover, unless there is something else supporting this method, it will often fail. It is a lot to ask anyone with experience to control their passions completely in the heat of the moment, so we can't ask teens without experience to do so. Chastity needs to be presented positively; scaring boys with STDs will only go so far.[10]

Mentoring will have very little value if the boy does not feel accepted and understood by his mentor; to understand him we must understand his world. Each boy' is a little different, but the preceding should express a general idea.

Mentors need to be aware of what may be happening at home. The family dimension of a boy's development is still very important. For example, teens who reported being highly satisfied with their relationship with parents were 2.7 times less likely to engage in sex than teens who had little satisfaction with their parental relationships,[11] and a strong parental bond usually means they start drinking later and have fewer problems with alcohol.[12] The largest study of teen religiosity noted that the differences in teen religiosity are directly proportional with the differences in parental religiosity – teens are as religious as their parents.[13]

The importance of family ties can also be brought home by an encounter I had with an older lady. I was travelling with a priest and we had stopped at a *Panera Bread* so he could see someone in spiritual direction; I sipped coffee and checked my e-mail in the meantime. A lady approached; she must have seen my collar.

"What do you think about the changes Bishop X is making?" (He had made some changes to emphasize the solemnity of the liturgy.)

"Well, all he is doing is in the mind of the Church..." As I started mentioning the specific changes, I mentioned something about the relationship of the mass with the temple sacrifices in ancient Israel. At this she exploded and, right there in the coffee shop, started yelling at me.

"That's wrong! God can't be a blood-thirsty God demanding the sacrifice of his son. The cross was a mistake. God sent his son to save us all but he didn't want him to die..." I will save you the rest of the tirade and heresies; by the end, her husband was trying to pull her away while I listened and responded quietly here and there.

I was a little exhausted after this. As I thought about it later that day, I realized what I should have answered: "Did you feel loved by your father?" My guess is that this was the origin of her errors. She rejected attributes of God that she thought corresponded to the negative aspects of her own father.

The boy relates with both mom and dad but usually prefers dad as the teen years progress. At 11 or 12, there is a strong attraction to the mother, but as he develops through puberty, she ceases to be the focal point for his decisions and is replaced by dad, and even more so by friends. The mother will often feel rejected when her son seems to be more distant, but this is proper maturing. Holding on to him too much is not healthy – it prevents him from developing as a Christian man. Moms need to know how support dad's work with the boy.

Of the two parents, dad now becomes all important as the boy is now self-conscious and sees himself as a man. Dad is the closest example of how to be a man. He can be rejected a bit by rebellion, but he needs to stick it out or he can lose his boy. Boys need to be taught to see the good in both parents, but this is more necessary with dad as they can usually list his faults more easily.

We can never replace parents and must always work with them. Parents are the primary educators of their children; a mentor is an extremely helpful assistant but cannot replace the key role of the parents. Never go against what parents tell a boy unless they counsel intrinsic evil (pre-marital sex, abortion, etc.). If in cases of prudence you disagree, bite your tongue before the boy, think about it calmly after, and if you still have a serious issue, speak with the parents, not the boy.

If the parents divorce or separate, boys feel anger, depression, blame, and despair. They can become quite worried with money or sexually hyperactive. They can compete with the parent of their own gender and succumb under the pressure of being the "man" of the house. Boys, especially if they are the oldest in the family, whose father is absent after the divorce have an even stronger temptation to make themselves equal rather than subservient to mom. They rarely see divorce as positive, the only exception being when they have seen or experienced physical violence in the home. There are two huge traps: blaming themselves or being so angry that they do nothing for an extended time period. It takes them a

SPIRITUALLY MENTORING TEENAGE BOYS

year or two to accept this reality and adapt to their new situation. Many do not learn to forgive, and they reject passage into adulthood. Others feel fear of failure in their own future marriage. [14]

Boys who come from single family homes or with step-parents often present us with a more difficult case. If their other natural parent died, the problems are often only practical because they sense that there was love. A boy can feel that a step-dad or step-mom is an unjust intruder in his family. They see the world from their perspective, not from an adult's. It is hard for such boys to get a proper image of God since they will tend to project their own parents' errors upon God. It is hard for them to accept authority because the basis of all authority – mom and dad, – have not lived out their authority properly (remember the 4th commandment refers to all authority as an extension of one's parents' authority). To the boy it seems like his parents made arbitrary choices that hurt him.

When a boy lacks a father, it is often good for him to have male models who take on some of the role of the father – a kind of substitute father. Sometimes it is best for a boy to focus on only one who has time to spend with him to help him develop his masculinity. Just as a natural father should not mentor his own son to avoid complicating relationships, if a mom asks you to take on such a role more formally you should find another mentor for the boy. Generally, a good mentor makes a good substitute dad but the 2nd is a much larger time commitment.

Whether in a family with both natural parents or with the various permutations we have been discussing, the key is always communication.[15] Communication to teens begins with attentive observation. To be able to observe one must "be present"; a parent must guarantee their discreet presence to our sons. "Discreet" because this presence should not be the same as it was when they were children. Observing does not mean insistently watching over, scrutinizing, or judging, which makes teenage boys nervous. Observing does not mean immediately looking for explanations of causes to make diagnoses and provide accelerated interpretations. Observing means to be present and know what is happening in his life so as to help him. It is good that he knows you and his parents are observing and present because a teen can feel forgotten or unimportant if they feel their parents take no interest in their lives. Mentors should begin communication with observation although they probably won't see as much as mom.

A parent needs to know how to listen. True listening is a profound exercise, and it is difficult both for parents and for children. When a parent habitually pays attention to his son only to be able to contradict him, correct him, point out his defects, or immediately tell him what he thinks he needs, he is not listening to him; he is simply fighting his own private battle. At times mentors will have to help the boys to accept their parents, imperfect as they are. Perhaps listening is not their strong point, but there are other ways which they show their love. It is important to help the boys learn to listen, not to be taken away by their passions and learn to speak about certain issues instead of arguing.

A parent should try to know their son. In modern times, a pseudo-psychological tendency has arisen to try to interpret everything, to try to find necessarily an explanation for all behavior and movement, for every word. Yet, interpretations are often mistaken because of lack of sufficient objective data about *this* teen; hence, erroneous concepts can be developed. Logically, this worsens relations, since such interpretation becomes prejudice and stereotype. Both parents and teens can jump to conclusions very easily. Teens should get to know their parents very well; but also help their parents get to know them. At times they may feel judged or feel like their parents do not understand or trust them – this is an unfortunate part of fallen nature.

Parents often need to learn to *not* act. Many times parents ask what to do, how to behave with their sons in such-and-such circumstance, and how to avoid making mistakes at critical moments. Many times, knowing how to act is very simple: "not acting" but "letting him act." Not acting is more difficult than acting even though it may not seem that way (not acting may seem like indifference but is radically different). Indeed, the most spontaneous response is often to react, to try to do something, especially when getting the sensation that sons are about to make mistakes or that they have not yet mature enough to confront a given situation. The fact is, the more a parent intervenes, the less initiative is often taken by the son. If failure isn't disastrous – losing a limb, flunking a grade of school, or a mortal sin – often the lessons learned from failure may be greater than the success would have been. (This principle can be called depth-confidence, and its application to mentoring comes later.) Boys should know that their parents are not born with all the solutions. They need to work together with their parents to make certain situations work.

Whatever parents do should be accompanied by encouragement. Encouragement is different from praise. Encouragement comes ahead of time. It consists in providing support for children in their efforts even before they undertake them. It means supporting them above and beyond the results attained, and especially when results are lacking. It means esteeming and respecting unconditionally. It means seeing the positive aspects of an adolescent's behavior, rather than underlining mistakes. Praise, on the other hand, is often aimed at obtaining from children what parents are hoping for. It comes after the fact. It leads to competitiveness and to the attitude that behavior is acceptable when it brings esteem from others. Encouragement leads children to take action without excessive, erroneous focus on the expectations of their parents. Boys need help discovering forms of encouragement that their parents have for them.

Despite some obvious differences between mentoring and parenting, such methodology often applies very well for us too: observe, listen, know the boy, and know when and how to act, and encourage. At times, we also need to help these aspects in the parent-child relationship – usually from the boy's side but possibly from the parents' side. A mentor needs to penetrate both friends and family to have a lasting impact on the boy. These environments both help make him who he is, and are the first places he can begin to change for Christ.

A Teen's Spiritual Life

Since one main focus of mentoring is the teen's spiritual development, we need to realize the spiritual steps a boy naturally makes during these years. From the openness to the world, originating in the other aspects of adolescent development we just spoke about, the flame of faith can easily be smothered. The teenage years bring a certain birth and fullness to religious ideals but they can also bring difficulties: individualism, perfectionism, doubts, and rationalism.

Spiritual life – according to certain authors – begins as a child develops the sense of being a son or daughter of God. About age 13 or 14 boys solidify their idea of God so they need to possess a true image of God before this period. If their parents are far from perfect, you need to help form this image right because God is often perceived as a super-parent. Teens project and amplify what they see in their parents. (Obviously he is more than that, but psychologically he is often perceived this way.)

Religious ideals appear in all of their beauty during puberty. A profound desire develops to fulfill these ideals, ideals that previously were merely attractive. The adolescent boy becomes ever more aware of the relationship that exists between him and society. Such religious ideals are also expressed in hero worship even if it is of a sports star. Such a relationship with society and with heroes can be elevated to the spiritual level.

As a child, a boy finds little difficulty in accepting and practicing the religious ideas of adults. Teens, because they feel like adults, ask about the reasons for things and think about the explanations given. Religion moves from a necessity to a desire: faith becomes personal. During this period, mentors need to be able to give boys profound reasons for their faith, even if they don't initially understand everything explained to them. Being Catholic means God should be the center of his life, especially at such a key moment. We offer mentoring to resolve these questions and so he can serve God and his neighbor.

The adolescent's psychological self-centeredness, combined with their altruistic and idealistic nature, often leads to a semi-messianic attitude. This is positive because the boy sees his action as essential for mankind's salvation and directs his life accordingly, but need be channeled to avoid egotism. The youth leader and other adult volunteers are your allies in channeling the boys. Emphasize what is true – a personal, transcendent mission in life – while directing it within the dynamics of God's plan – Christ invites you to participate in his messianic mission and his intimate life – and with a communal dimension – you will share this mission with others, forming a single force with them for salvation.

The adolescent begins to perceive larger-scale spiritual needs. Mentors need to clarify this, distinguishing between true spiritual life (holiness) and moral perfectionism. This should help the teen distance himself from any budding scrupulosity, moralism, and harsh judgment. This should also help with any inevitable crises that arise from the disjointed moral life of some.

Certain spiritual issues must be addressed in mentoring or elsewhere: sin, the mystery of the hereafter, and the difficulty in receiving help from religion for resolving personal problems. This issues need to be dealt with early because between the ages of 15 and 16, the problems accumulate fast: failure to observe religious practice, rejection of liturgical acts, and conflicts between science and religion.

Given these natural strengths and weakness in a teen's spiritual life, certain religious practices are needed to strengthen him on the journey. Whatever happens in their life, they need to stay close to the sacraments of confession and the Eucharist. Various prejudices and fears could lead them to distance themselves from confession at an age when they need it the most. Frequent reception of the Eucharist and confession (along with personal responsibility) is the most effective "remedy" for the mood swings characteristic of this phase in life.

Since the teen is at an age when he internalizes experiences and opens up to others, it is clear that this is a particularly propitious moment for fostering a relationship with Christ in faith. Personal meditation must become spontaneous and habitual for the adolescent. Now that he is breaking some of his emotional ties with his family, he needs more than ever to discover the Christ the Friend and establish a real, continuous, and intimate friendship with him. He feels a great need for these traits of friendship, and he will have difficulty discovering them fully in his human friends.

Now that we have seen a quick overview of adolescent psychology, you should realize one thing: mentoring is not psychology and you will not be a psychologist after reading this. When you encounter certain psychological difficulties while mentoring, try to help them spiritually continue forward with the help of God's grace, from the reality where they are. When the case requires it, speak to the parents about possible psychological help. (Try to recommend psychologists who have a Christian understanding of man, or they might further trouble the boy. Catholic psychologists can be found at www.catholictherapist.com.)

The various stages of adolescent psychology in diverse areas are summarized in Appendix B. They are put alongside the various areas of formation that teens should receive (also by stages).

As a teen progresses from early adolescence (where he starts differentiating himself from girls) to the last stages (where he is defining himself), radical changes happen. Physiological and emotional changes are the most obvious ones, but others can have a more profound effect. His relationships with both friends and family begin to be based on true sociability not just mere likeability. Girls change from cootie monsters to the other attractive enough to spend his life with. And finally, he goes from mechanical religious practice to a deep relationship based on religious ideals. Mentors need to accompany teens in all these changes to set them on the right path for life.

8. FORMATION: DEVELOPMENT OF THE PERSON'S DIMENSIONS

Now we move into a whole new area, switching form psychology to the formation that is appropriate, given what we learned from psychology. If we want to form someone, especially a teenager, we have to know them more than the formation we want to give. This will be divided in the four areas of integral formation: Intellectual, Human, Spiritual, and Apostolic.[1]

> Parents, professors, adults... we should all feel the challenge of forming the future of society – youth – the light of great and perennial ideals. Formation in love for God, for the sake of the one ideal that lasts forever and unifies the life of a believer: God Our Lord, Our Father, Our Creator."[2]

Three ideas guide all formation. (1) We can never be satisfied with the status quo; no matter where the boy may be, there is always room for improvement. (2) We need to form a complete human being, not just one aspect or one virtue such as willpower. (3) We teach doctrinal material and the proper use of one's mind; we educate the human faculties and the social and moral virtues; and we form the spiritual-religious and apostolic dimensions of each person.

This chapter will examine each of the four areas on its own. This division is not to indicate progressive stages but parts of a whole that each boy needs to form. You may want to read Appendix B later since it gives a year-by-year summary of this chapter and the last one.

Intellectual Formation

We disagreed about everything. We were each a member of opposing political parties. However, Mr. Beateau was not like most teachers. His classes were filled with debate. Students would go home and look up material beyond the required readings to prove their point. For two years, he was my teacher for honors Social Studies and my debate coach. Despite the fact that I don't remember most of his classes, I think he was probably the teacher who did the most to form me. Instead of requiring that we listen to the teacher and memorize, he taught me to think.

The kids we mentor will probably get the content elsewhere – mentoring is not teaching the Bible and the catechism – but so often they will lack this inquisitive nature, this love for truth, and the tools to reach it. As an adult, this intellectual virtue may be more valuable than a whole year of scholastic material received. Nonetheless, you should have a decent catechetical knowledge so you can answer questions if they arise. While catechizing, avoid our tendency to intellectualize our faith.

We need to help the boys form good mental habits: reflection, analysis, synthesis, and judgment. You can draw examples from your specific line of work here as most adult jobs involve a decent amount of these four habits. A well-developed imagination is an exceptional tool for fostering a rich interior life and an intimate relationship with the Holy Spirit, who imprints the image of Christ within us. Our techniques need to be adapted to the teens' age and psychology. The mentoring we offer needs to be intelligible, attractive, and easily assimilated by the boy. In mentoring, this area is downplayed because it should generally be provided by the activities of the group.

Human Formation

Human formation involves the whole person. The temptation here is focus on the externals. Human formation is first of all about the boys' inner world of sentiments, will, passions, conscience, and character, and only about social virtues by extension. The ultimate goal of human formation is maturity; the teens are all on the path. Maturity can be defined as constancy in love. When one is mature, his decisions are conscious and thoughtful, his emotional forces are mastered by reason, and his life is based on principles and convictions. A mature man can give himself constantly to others with an open and unselfish heart. Obviously, a mature man is not selfish or individualistic. To reach that human maturity, teens must learn to control and channel emotions and passions, to develop character, to have an upright conscience, and develop certain external virtues as a result.

In educating a boy's sentiments, the goal is to place them at the service of the will and the intellect enlightened by supernatural faith. Sentiments can be defined as reactions of the psyche when affected by any stimuli. Teens need to learn to give the various sentiments a proper hierarchy. Sentiments tend to be inconsistent, and hence formation built on them is like the man who built his house on sand. The rain and winds came, and everything was lost.

Sentimentalism is a huge enemy of solid formation, but sentiments can also help. They give impetus, like the sail of a ship, as long as they are controlled by the intellect of the captain and the will of the steersman. The point of departure for forming the passions is to keep in mind that they cannot be uprooted, but must rather be channeled appropriately. The force of passion, which can go off track in the direction of pride and sensuality, needs to be reoriented to help one reach the ideal of formation, to master oneself, to be transformed into Christ, to work effectively for Christ's kingdom. Sentiments complete a person.

To live as a person rather than a beast, a man must master his lower faculties with his intellect and will. Although we are enlightened by our senses, our intellect, and most of all by faith; actually living an upright Christian life depends primarily on the will. The will is a pivotal faculty. A well-formed will is the key to all subsequent development in spiritual, human, and intellectual formation. Lack of will can become the guillotine of all efforts and aspirations toward perfection. There is a struggle, therefore, to make sure those in formation do not meet up with definitive defeats, and will power is an indispensable weapon for avoiding that.

'Besides differences in outer appearance, character, one's "own way of being"," is what sets one person apart from another. In human life, character should not be considered something akin to fate, forcing a person to act in predetermined ways. While we live according to our character every day, a teenager is forming his character every day; he is becoming the man he will be. (We too can form our character but with more difficulty than teens.) Each one has a different personality, family, and experience, but all need to be aided to form a character that reflects Christ. Evangelization begins with those who reflect Christ. In his character, a mentor should help each boy to balance and order the various faculties.

A central area of human formation is helping a boy from his conscience. Our age has long lost the sense of sin, but now it has even lost the sense of criteria at all. People no longer argue that a sin is OK, but that there are no criteria to judge right and wrong. Society cannot long survive this way. We speak of freedom and human rights; then we go and kill through abortion, euthanasia, and embryonic stem cell research. A man claims maturity as his guiding star but acts like a mere child, following the winds of media, fashion, and advertising.

To create boys with Christian consciences, we need to go against the culture of relativism. The moral values that regulate human behavior are essential today. Yet as a base for receiving those values, they need upright consciences whose norms of conduct are founded on the objective law man discovers and recognizes, with the help of right reason, in his human nature. The boys need to learn to reject anything contrary to the spirit of Christ.

We need to help them become men in a culture that wants to treat them as boys. Youth ministry is not just creating a fun environment to entertain them. Instead it should transform each boy into the image God has of him. If we help them become men, I think that gratitude and a lifelong commitment to Christ's Church would be the logical consequence.

In the development of the internal human aspects, they will tend to manifest a noble and attractive soul in the external virtues: honesty, loyalty, fidelity, gratitude, justice, and fortitude, to name a few. In today's culture, we cannot assume they exist. The first work of a mentor is laying the foundations in the interior so that the boy can develop such virtues exteriorly.

External human virtues, if lived in balance become a social "presentation card." So often such "presentation cards" today are simply a façade; if however we base these external virtues on the internal, they become a real means to evangelization and helping others.

Mentors should help teens see which virtues need to be worked on and how they can be developed. No boy is going to arrive as an ideal specimen; each needs some work. There is a certain prudence involved in picking the right virtue for each boy at each moment. The more foundational virtues need to be cultivated first, if one isn't honest, one's fidelity doesn't matter. The three keys are honesty, fortitude, and charity. Once they have the foundations, the virtues need to be taught in a way that goes beyond the particular circumstances the boy is living in now. We need to give him practical hints for living them today but always with principles that can be applied in different circumstances.

The human virtues provide a base for God's grace to transform the teen into the saint God sees him as. We start deep inside and work outwards so the external virtues are made of rock rather than paper-thin. Without control of emotions and a well-formed conscience, good manners are only a show.

Spiritual Formation

A teen must experience God as a friend, answering his questions and inviting him to carry out a great project. To have such an experience, they need an upright conscience, freely chosen dependence on God, an interior life, a life of grace, and certain virtues.

Teens can encounter God in their conscience. Conscience was also part of human formation: there it regarded proper judgments, while here it regards the place of encounter with God as friend. All of man's ethical effort is equivalent to a personal, friendly, and filial response to this questioning from a God who is father and friend. Conscience begins to deform, however, the moment it ceases to be the voice of the friend who asks, invites and suggests, and instead becomes a nuisance, baby-sitter, or judge. Man is fundamentally open to the transcendent absolute (i.e. God) as the value that surpasses and encompasses all else, not just as one value among many. We reach fulfillment to the degree we fill that openness to God, allowing him to transform our life.

The most fundamental element of man is his dependence on God. Man would cease to exist were God to stop thinking of him. Without God, or apart from him, man would be nothing. This gives rise to a series of consequences. One of these consequences is giving God first place in one's life. Moreover, this is in strict keeping with what he wants for each person. Human freedom could have the final word by drawing away from God, thus falling into absurd contradiction. But freedom exists to love; we are *"free with the very freedom of the gift."*[3] Man expresses his freedom fully giving himself to God and others – this is the basis of any spiritual life and any apostolate.

Adolescence is an ideal time to develop an interior life. Interior life is more than just saying prayers; it is having a relationship with God through grace and the theological virtues of faith, hope, and charity. We don't need to complicate it: when one has a good interior life, it is real, natural, and personal. As a boy lives it, he should slowly develop the same sentiments as Christ. It is an attitude of trusting, filial love that moves us to keep the attitude of a beloved son in our relationship to God our Father.

All spiritual life is living the life of grace, but this grace is received first by frequent reception of the sacraments and second by living in God's presence. This life of grace would evidently imply a habit of regular prayer to maintain it; boys need help to fall in love with Jesus. The world imposes a rationalistic view of everything but we need to offer the boys a supernatural vision.

Spiritual formation still needs to get down to brass tacks and help the boy form particular virtues. Unbreakable adherence to God's will, which goes beyond following orders, will allow their lives to take on the proper direction. Exteriorly, boys need to live charity beyond mere helpfulness and zeal that drives every action towards extending Christ's kingdom. Finally, self-denial and sacrifice (obviously, within limits) are great instruments towards achieving any spiritual goal.

As we accompany teens, we must help them develop such principles, attitudes, and virtues. With these set, each boy should have what it takes to become a saint.

Apostolic Formation

Apostolate is not an accessory, but should be the manifest consequence of the boy's faith. Everything we give him should be in order to serve; our freedom exists to give. All Christians, by Baptism and Confirmation, are called to share in Christ's mission to the world. This impetuous for the laity to become apostles was renewed by Vatican II: apostolate is not just for priests and nuns.

It is not just spending a few hours of their time on more or less interesting apostolic activities. First, each adolescent must be aware that he can be an apostle: one who is so convinced by Christ that he dedicates his whole life to leading others to him. As a boy gets older, the specific apostolates tend to be what keeps him united to the club or youth ministry program – without them it can become one more thing in his agenda.

As time goes on, his responsibility in these apostolates should grow as well. This area should never be neglected; he needs to be already into an apostolate before the idea of leaving your youth group for something else more "fun" even enters his head. From the first time he comes, he should be introduced to regular monthly or weekly apostolate. This is not just a practical suggestion to avoid losing numbers; it is a concrete way to help them be generous. Generosity is the center of apostolic formation.

Apostolate also helps them to go outside themselves and see people in need. It takes them out of their shell to experience Christ in others. Boys cannot mature fully in a bubble. I still remember one night in college when I went down to feed the homeless with an ecumenical group of friends. We were 2 blocks from where I would transfer buses when I was 14 – often I would even stop for a bit after school at the main branch of the public library there. It really surprised when one of the girls said that her Christian parents would not approve of her being downtown. I think she was 20! It is still hard for me to understand how such a person will never be able to know the real world.

This means that little by little the mentor will need to form this apostolic personality in each boy with enthusiasm, patience, and determination, taking every opportunity to enkindle apostolic zeal and to uproot the self-centeredness hidden behind a false conception that Christianity is individualistic and minimalist. Most mentoring sessions should mention apostolate.

Thus we conclude the overview of Integral Formation applied to mentoring. I include Appendix B at the end, which summarizes the various psychological stages and the corresponding formation. If the intellectual, human, spiritual and apostolic formation still seem a little vague, don't worry as they will reappear in other places; the four areas of formation are a good way of diving the goal in mentoring and will be a guiding light throughout. We begin with human and intellectual formation, which are the base for spiritual and apostolic formation.

9. Ten Pedagogical Principles

Ted was a quiet boy, who liked reading. His father was reasonably rich but alcoholic, beating him regularly. His dad always wanted him to be a sports star, but he was not the most coordinated. He never felt the love of his father. Finally, in college, he managed to captain the sailing team. All was not well as his father despised his idea to major in Classics; saying he "almost puked" at the thought.[1] That's an example of *bad* pedagogy.

Ted Turner went on to be the billionaire owner of TV stations. However, he had 3 wives, was diagnosed with psychological disorders, and attacked Catholics for wearing ashes on Ash Wednesday. He is reliving the childhood that was robbed from him.

All adults, in some way, relive their adolescence. The way we help them experience will set them for life. Youth are the future of families, of society, and of the Church so each of us takes on an important role when we become a mentor. St Thomas Aquinas said "a small error in the beginning will be a grave error at the end."[2] We are working with boys at the beginning of their personality and their intellectual life.

A boy is like a young sapling, brimming with life, but which can be distorted and killed by the smallest change. Therefore it is essential for us to set them on the right path.

> To form is more than a concept or theory. It is to lead a person to his fulfillment and maturity, which is the same as orienting him towards the final goal of his life, towards his ideal, towards the will of God. To form is to contribute to building the new person in every human being.[3]

In other words, via mentoring we seek to transform each boy into the new man in Christ.

When our task amounts to nothing less than forming the hearts and consciences of the next generation, we cannot improvise. We need maturity and diligence. A good mentor tries to deepen his understanding and always stay up-to-date. Both in the practice by asking other experienced mentors (watching and asking questions) and in theory through good books that explain the Catholic faith, the spiritual life or formation (reading). Nothing can make up for lack of preparation.

To accomplish such a noble goal, I want to outline 10 pedagogical principles that are the building blocks for mentoring. All of these principles are means to impart formation; while some are also goals, here they are presented as principles of formation.

1. Personalized Formation

Each soul should be known thoroughly and completely: likes, preferences, talents, interests, people he gets along with and people he doesn't. Each soul should be offered help and challenges tailored to his talents and personality. You need to be familiar with each boy and know him personally. In this respect our task is never done; we can always do more to know the boys we direct.

Each mentoring session needs to be the best one for that

particular person. From what we have already seen, we know that each boy is a unique creation of God. Wipe clean the slate and give each teen 100% attention and union with the Holy Spirit. There is no magic recipe that applies to everyone.[4]

Today there is a lot of talk of the changes that technology makes to pedagogy. Because mentoring is personalized – both one-on-one and interested in the boy as a complete person – it goes above and beyond these changes. I don't have a crystal ball to see what will happen with e-books, the internet, or wired classrooms to change how formation happens in the next 20 years. But no matter what changes are made here the human person remains the same, so pedagogy will be essentially the same.

2. Conviction and the Mentor's Ability to Guide

At first glance, conviction may seem to mean leaving the soul on his own to reach the goals he considers best for himself. This is the approach of those who reject mentoring or spiritual direction, appealing to the well-known argument that it is just a "tool for manipulation". They misunderstand mentoring since they forget the chief premise of respect for an individual's freedom. These people promote a false freedom, where mentoring does not a lead a soul to God (on top of the mountain) and is non-directive (points out various animals and trees on the mountainside as you pass them). How can this be the answer? Unfortunately, this misunderstanding is widespread. It is one thing to coerce someone to do something against their will, it is quite another to offer guidance that help's the boy form himself so he can discover God's will. We cannot shy away from leading these boys to become the men God created them to be.

Being directive does not mean that you decide God's will for the teen. Rather, you are there to help him discover it. In this sense, good mentoring is both directive and non-directive.[5] This explains why at times I use the word "accompany" to refer to mentoring and at other times I use "form" – each one expresses one side of the same whole.

Purely non-directive mentoring will often lead a boy to follow the path of society or his passions. In fact, some modern "expert" psychologists are the foremost promoters of this view of one on-one spiritual formation. However, no matter how many "experts" together with our society promote a hedonistic lifestyle, where you unleash your passions and live according to them, they can't make this the right way for man to live. One of the earliest Church documents (from about AD 100) says: "Don't remove your hand from your son or daughter, but from their youth teach them the fear of God."[6] As well, the ancient Christian writer Origen praises those who remove temptations from the passions of youth such as those improperly dressed.[7] The tradition of the Church is a better guide than the ambivalent "experts" – to do otherwise, we sin by omission. (Some boys will be able to make it perfectly well without mentoring, but not every boy.)

An adolescent, more or less unconsciously, looks for guidance amid his needs and uncertainties, thus showing the innate desire everyone has to be oriented—as a constitutive need of human nature—towards his goal. Little by little the person gains confidence and awareness of what he possesses to help him live a life based on freely accepted principles.

3. Knowing Oneself, Accepting Oneself, Bettering Oneself

The admonition *Know yourself* was carved on the temple portal at Delphi, as testimony to a basic truth to be adopted as a minimal norm by those who seek to set themselves apart from the rest of creation as "human beings", that is, as those who "know themselves".[8]

Knowing yourself is the first step in formation. From self-knowledge, a boy moves on to acceptance, to learning to appreciate and thank God for one's gifts. Acceptance also means acknowledging one's limitations without envy of other's gifts. In all self-discovery an optimistic realism needs to be sought – and a positive attitude kept. If not, it can cause trauma and, sometimes, a drifting away from God, who doesn't seem just in distributing gifts.

The effort to better oneself will be seen as a logical requirement of having failings, shortcomings, and falls. It is not enough to say, "That's the way I am." A leader is whoever wants to be a leader, as long as he recognizes his own errors. The day he says, "This is far enough," is the day he begins to go backwards.[9]

4. Motivation

Boys need motivations, deep ones that they grasp onto as an essential part of their life. Mentors need to ensure they have these motivations before we demand from them and never demand beyond where their motivations can carry them. Some examples of such motivations: zeal for souls, love of Christ, awareness of God's love, helping the Church, building up the body of Christ, becoming a leader of souls, changing the world, being a good child of Mary, etc. Motivation implies that we implant positive motivations (love), not fears; fear fades as soon as the object feared is no longer present, while love continues on. If we are ever tempted to get negative, remember Christ said: "There is joy before the angels of God over one sinner who repents."[10]

5. Preventative System

This system was expounded by St John Bosco: teach kids all the ways to have good fun. Don't control them, but make the positive environment so attractive they willingly choose it. This system implies being always on the watch, one step ahead. For teenagers, life is something new; for you it is a school for observing and teaching. Vigilance shows authentic love for them, especially their souls. A mentor should always present the positive path but he cannot force it upon the boy.

6. Atmosphere of Trust and Confidentiality

This atmosphere is even more important in light of the uncertainties and insecurities of adolescents. They should feel "comfortable" with the adult volunteers and teen leaders in youth ministry, certain that they will be accepted and understood whenever they confide in them. There is no denying that the soul knows that what he is told is for his own good, and that it will help him overcome fears and insecurities. Teens need certainty of their mentor's confidentiality. The breaking of that confidentiality, whether out of misunderstanding or indiscretion, usually means a definitive breaking off of the formative process. (Certain extreme cases to be dealt with later are exceptions to this rule.)

7. Discipline

Discipline means an ordering of the faculties; not being a drill sergeant. If you have to enforce discipline externally, it means the boys have yet to internalize it. Mentors need to begin with the conviction that inner discipline is what makes integral, harmonious formation possible. Outer discipline is little more than a mirroring of the inner and, at the same time, a reinforcement of it.

8. Work with Leaders

The simple fact is that we all have limited time to work with the boys – they are only present at youth ministry so many hours, we usually have a separate full-time job, etc. We want the boys to come to mentoring with the best preparation. Some of the boys are leaders, so what you form in them, you form partially in the others by extension. By "leaders" I don't mean some special group, but simply those boys who influence the others. Prioritize them without neglecting the others, and then you will be able to offer more formation to the boys in the little time you have available to mentor them. Practically, this means that if you don't have time to see every boy individually each month, you can make sure you see the top few monthly, and see some of the others every 2 months.

9. Teamwork

Mentoring, as was stated in the introduction, is by far most effective when it is combined with some kind of group-based youth ministry. You cannot work separately from them. You need to be constantly exchanging ideas, seeing what themes the boys are touching in the group, asking for any boys who have certain talents or difficulties that might be good to review in mentoring.

10. Christ-centeredness

In pedagogy we can't forget that the focus of Christian anthropology is Christ. "[St] Paul's exhortations were not so much to virtue as to the following of Christ."[11] Even more than following Christ, "Christ is at once the pattern of holiness and its principal inspiration,"[12] so every virtue is presented as embodied in Jesus Christ, not abstractly on its own. Virtue is a power of man; but Christ is the perfect man with all power. Christ is the model of *every* virtue.

Only those who assimilate and adopt as their own the personality of Christ – true God and true man – can form themselves integrally. And we need to remember that true supernatural efficacy stems from grace. Nothing is achieved without grace for Jesus said, "apart from me you can do nothing."[13]

These ten principles present a pedagogical framework in which mentoring is inserted. Mentoring works in an environment where the boy is positively and personally welcomed and directed towards the one true model, Jesus Christ.

10. THE MENTOR'S ROLE IN PEDAGOGY

After going over 10 general principles of pedagogy, we need to see how and where your role as a mentor fits in. Pedagogy gives a general outline for all those who form teens, but a mentor has a specific role in their formation. Mentoring is an interpersonal relationship that begins with one person – the mentor – and is addressed to another person – the boy – individually. It is a relationship of conviction and personal development that enables the boy to embrace a series of values, and reject other anti-values because the values are objectively superior. It is a system based on a philosophy of values and the philosophy of personalism. Others who work with youth ministry focus on organizing events or talking to groups, but mentoring is individualized.

To achieve the individual formation we seek, mentoring requires the full participation of both the mentor and the teen. He picks up immediately whether a mentor is fully dedicated to him, to his spiritual development, to seeking his good alone. A good mentor knows each person in-depth and uses the most appropriate approach with each one. You need to gauge the boy's interest. You can only help him form himself if he wants to.

Mentoring is accompaniment but also formation – you must desire the teen's good and his development. You can lead him to his own good if you are completely focused. Seek at every moment to influence, enrich, orient, and bring to fullness the personality of the souls entrusted to him through the presentation of materials, the embodiment of virtue and attitudes, and the assimilation of principles.

The teen must want formation. Individual freedom means the desired results are not always achieved, no matter your effort. The soul needs to give his all to reach the goal. Present the boy with great models and ideals so that he will want to form himself.

As a mentor, you need to always keep your role in mind; you are the personal trainer on the youth ministry team. You often achieve the most profound results but only because the others have led the Gospel reflection and organized the service project. We need to give the boys depth-confidence, and usually the mentor is the best one to do this. Before we get to this depth-confidence, we need to review eight attitudes that are particularly important for mentors. Few have all these attitudes naturally – in fact many seem paradoxical. We must all strive to achieve them so we can mentor boys well.

8 Basic Attitudes of a Good Mentor

1. Practice What You Preach:

Youth will follow what we practice way more than they follow what we preach; teens clearly sense the authenticity of their mentors. For this reason, our example is the first principle a mentor must live; he should obtain the teens' admiration and desire to imitate him thanks to his lifestyle. Authentic leadership is persuasion through example. It is useless to try to fool them. We are working with teens that have generous hearts, and our influence as mentors is often definitive, for good or ill. Boys will pick up everything, even though this is often an unconscious process: boys can see through the façade.

2. Faith in the Mission and Common Sense:

A good mentor is aware that he is building on the action of grace. Based on that awareness, he should try to spread love for the ideal by living a life of deep prayer and sacrifice that guarantees the divine fruitfulness of his action. This confidence in the grace of God and faith in his action in the formation of the youth is very important, but we cannot be ignorant to the fact that He needs our active and intelligent cooperation. Common sense keeps us planted on the ground as we contemplate the mission.

3. Kindness and Insistence:

A noble heart always shows kindness and understanding. We have to know, with prudence, the right balance between being gentle and firm; which varies from boy to boy. To have boys accept formation, we first need to show them love. If they see our love, they can respond with love. We need to know how to reach the heart of each boy so that we can orient his soul, and to do so we need to accept him as he is.

4. Patience and Constancy:

A mentor molds people; he is working with clay. Never forget that you are not dealing with things or fixed laws, but rather with free individuals brimful of virtues and defects of passion and sentiment. This means you must demand without suffocating, and struggle without disheartening.

5. The Proper Use of Authority:

A mentor must know how to guide without being domineering. A mentor is an authentic leader when he convinces others through the truth of his principles, the height and beauty of his ideals, and the power of his witness of self-giving.

6. Serenity, Reflection, and Self-Mastery:

A good mentor should never be overwhelmed by circumstances. Serenity instills courage in others during moments of greater struggle and upheaval. These virtues define his depth of leadership. Learning to control nervous tension is necessary if one wishes to be respected by teens.

7. Universality:

A good mentor always tries to create an atmosphere of universality and harmony amid the constant reactions of liking or disliking a person based on their behavior or way of being. By this I mean that you have to treat kids equally and fairly – this doesn't necessarily mean the same. Don't impose your criteria on them, but get them to accept them with love. Never disdain or think less of them. Love them all without signs of preference.

8. Maturity:

You need to come to teens with maturity but need to bring maturity out of them. If you are not mature in your dealings with teens, you can never expect them to be. The maturity of a particular teen can vary five years forward or five years back from their biological age based on the day and the issue. Use their most mature moments as a guideline.

You will usually get the best response if you treat them like adults. We have certain rules of politeness we use every day with other adults; unfortunately they are often thrown out talking to teens. At times, you will realize they are not, but the solution is not to regress to treating them like kids, but to help them express what is going on inside of them in adult terms. This way the relationship will be much more fruitful for them and for you as well.[1]

Depth-Confidence

Boys need help to become men. If we treat them as five-year-olds, we will get a five-year-old's response. If we treat them like men and give them confidence (i.e. responsibility), they will become men and rise up to the challenge. I want to review what depth-confidence is, why teens are ready for it, the process, and the effects.

My friend David Murray tells a story about going back to his old youth club in Ireland. A 12 or 13 year old greeted him at the door. He suggested his kids would like the place and wanted to check it out. The boy offered to show him the place.

As they toured he was the model of politeness. Nobody else was there. David complimented him afterwards only to here that the boy was in charge of public relations every Wednesday from the end of school to dinner.[2]

Would you be willing to do that? Obviously not the first day. However, when we mentor boys, we need to slowly develop a sense of mutual trust. The toughest part on the side of the mentor is when we have to trust the boy beyond what we can control. This is where you trust him to do something knowing he may fail. You trust him to organize an apostolate; you trust him with the keys to the center like in David's story; or you trust him to direct a group of younger boys on a retreat.

If a boy is to become a leader as an adult, at some point he must be given this trust. The challenge will be preparing him for it, knowing when you can give it to him, and being there to help him after a fall. To prepare him, you need to trust him with little things. He needs to accomplish small resolutions between mentoring sessions and these should grow slowly till trusting him with depth-confidence seems the natural next step. Resolutions not only serve to improve this or that little aspect, but need to be part of a boy's transformation into an apostle of Christ. The practical section will develop this aspect.

Don't say "but they're teens!" Recent psychological evidence indicates that from puberty on, age is not a good judge of competence. When given a 140 question test of adult competence, teens 13-17 scored only 2% below adults.[3] Therefore, many of the teens you are dealing with should have the competence to merit your depth-confidence. In fact, our brains seem to reach their maximum potential during our teen years,[4] so in some respects those you mentor may be more capable of many things than adults.

It should seem more or less obvious when a major responsibility should be offered to a boy; it is often earlier than you expect, so be ready. Inevitably, he will fail one of his first times. Nobody is perfect. You need to let him fall – what you have given him at this stage should not involve a fatal fall if he fails. (Usually a fall at this level will mean that a small apostolate flops, a little money is spent uselessly, or his team members and friends can't go play basketball because he forgot to reserve the courts.) The temptation is to grab him before he falls, but this takes away a huge learning opportunity. By this stage, the boy should trust you enough to come back to talk after. Now you need to help him see why he fell and improve for the future. Take him back a step, but don't lose all trust in him – nine times out of ten, his failure is not based on something serious but rather a simple mistake.

Getting boys to the stage of depth-confidence is tough, but worth every drop of sweat. From here, you can move him out towards being an adult Christian, where he no longer looks to you to give him apostolic tasks but to guide him in the apostolate he freely assumes. One of the greatest joys a mentor can have is to see a teen leave teenage dependence and become an adult. Mentoring will no longer have much purpose but can be transformed more along the lines of spiritual direction. This is the path to make saints.

The main effect of depth-confidence is helping teens move from children to adults. So many today want to protect teens from every possible danger and effort. However many teen problems and the classic teen rebellion may stem from overprotection. Often such actions are affirmations by the teen that he is an adult. If he succeeds with real responsibilities, he has already proven he is an adult, so such actions become silly. Depth-confidence transforms him from a child to an adult.

Allen and Allen build on its transformative effect in *Escaping Endless Adolescence*. They list offering an adult-like responsibility as the first way for teens to become adults.[5] Depth-confidence is the attitude the adult must have so that a teen can take this step. Doing something that is really adult helps teens avoid trying to become pseudo-adults by other means such as drinking, sex, or crime. Not every job or volunteer opportunity is adult; some expand the pseudo-adult bubble. Real adult responsibilities, according to the Allens, are those that change other people's lives, that include real responsibility, that others depend on, that teens freely chose, and that don't give too much spending cash (hence often proper volunteer work is best). What we want for our teens today in youth ministry paradoxically includes all these elements. It isn't always easy to find the right responsibility for each teen, but the results are worth the effort. I think that helping teens become adults within the Church will be the seed for many to dedicate their life to ministry, and help the rest live their faith actively.

I still remember how my dad showed me depth-confidence. My dad is a property manager, so my job as a teenager was cleaning, painting, and repairing rental properties. When I was young, my dad would always work with me on the same job; later he would be working on the same house but somewhere else; then he would drop me off at 9am on Saturday morning, show me what needed doing and say he would be back with lunch; and by the time I was 16, Saturday morning would begin by giving me three things: a list of work to be done, keys to the truck, and keys to the house I needed to work on. Depth-confidence doesn't come overnight, but it is a process that makes the boy into an independent young man.

With the desire to offer this confidence to teens and the eight attitudes, you should be able to see how you as a mentor fit into youth ministry. The two need to go hand in hand.

SPIRITUALITY AND PRAYER

Spiritual mentoring covers a broad range of the teenager's formation but it specializes in the spiritual life. This section explores teen spirituality. Teenage spirituality is similar to adult spirituality but is not the same. The four chapters are divided in two parts: the first two deal with a general outline and principle, while the latter two deal with prayer specifically.

11. INTRODUCTION TO THE SPIRITUAL LIFE FOR TEENS

Our whole life is one long path of growth towards the fullness that God has called us to in heaven, from sitting on mom's lap during mass till we receive anointing of the sick in a hospital bed. "There are no plains in the Spiritual life. We go uphill, or we go downhill."[1] But certain moments are special. The teen years are when faith either becomes personal or it is lost.

A personal prayer life, speaking with God and not just saying prayers, can begin during the teen years. This is probably the ideal time to begin it. The boy now has a personality and is sociable but has not solidified his ways like we adults have. If he develops a personal prayer life now, that will bode well for him throughout life. Developing their Christian personality, boys inevitably make choices. Their choices as teens define them as true Christians or E&C (Easter and Christmas) Catholics. At some point they have to embrace faith on their own, independent of their parents' prodding. For this they need to experience Jesus in prayer and others.

Changing from a parent-directed to a personal faith should be coupled with spiritual life. Faith is not just intellectual assent. Faith is adherence of our actions to Christ. A spiritual life nurtures our faith and keeps it fresh. Our spiritual life touches every aspect of our day-to-day. The spiritual life includes not only prayer, but also every dimension of friendship with God and the daily experience of following Jesus Christ.

Embarking on the spiritual life is like starting to climb a mountain. But what is the goal? The goal of spiritual life is holiness. We were made for God, for holiness. As St Augustine said, "our hearts are restless until they rest in you, O Lord."[2] Holiness is not about one's own efforts but about a gift from God. God's ultimate gift is love because "God is love,"[3] so holiness is love. To be holy is to be united with God, love Itself. As John Paul II put it, "Holiness is intimacy with God."[4]

Many think of holiness as listening to angels on harps or staying home every Friday night. St John Bosco teaches just the opposite: the holy boys have the most fun! A sullen boy is not holy. A holy boy is one who lives a full life (sports, jokes, games) and has a personal friendship with God which is so strong it overflows into love of neighbor. One does not need extraordinary circumstances to grow in holiness, just extraordinary love.[5] A boy can become holy on his sports team and at school; not just kneeling in church.

Christ is not only our best friend in striving for holiness, he is our model. Following Christ's example means adopting his moral framework. He provides the example of his disciples. How did he make choices? What was his hierarchy of values? Imitation involves study. So the teen needs to know him, especially in the Eucharist, in the Gospel, and on the Cross. Following upon this vision of holiness, a bunch of aspects follow logically. This chapter will focus on a basic outline and the means of the spiritual life. The next chapter will apply this outline. We conclude this section with two chapters on prayer.

A Basic Outline of the Spiritual Life

The beginning of any path to holiness begins with a

fundamental option: "I have set before you life and death, blessing and curse; therefore choose life, that you and your descendants may live."[6] Only God can make a teen holy, but the teen must cooperate. The fundamental option is to make that choice to cooperate with God and renew it daily. This simple option sets the foundation for one's life to know, love, and follow Christ. As they follow Christ, boys begin where we all did, but they progress through various stages faster since they don't yet have so much baggage. The main aids to progress are the theological virtues, love for Christ, obedience, Mary, and the human virtues.

After making this option, the boy is not home free, but must still wage a spiritual battle. The catechism teaches "The battle of prayer is inseparable from the necessary 'spiritual battle' to act habitually according to the Spirit of Christ: we pray as we live, because we live as we pray."[7] This battle is against the world, the flesh (including oneself), and the devil.

This battle has various stages.[8] The beginner stage is called the purgative stage, which purifies the soul. "In the spiritual life, *beginners* are those that habitually live in the state of grace and have a certain desire for perfection, but who have still attachments to venial sin and are exposed to fall now and then into grievous faults."[9] If one wants to run a marathon, the first days of training will be the hardest. To grow spiritually every person needs to get into shape. This is painful at the beginning because one needs to let go of certain things and get used to other elements. Hence it's called the purgative stage – although that name can be misleading in other contexts. The more advanced stages are the *illuminative* (doing good acts) and *unitive* (deep and peaceful union with God) stages. The names can be deceptive as the path in some ways becomes more difficult. The purgative, however, has purged the soul of anything directly evil. These divisions are general guidelines and in fact often two or three work in the soul at once. When it comes down to it, everyone is a beginner in one way or another.

The great spiritual director Thomas Dubay mentions that spiritual directors need to prepare generous souls to experience infused contemplation or the unitive way.[10] Since spiritual mentoring should lead to spiritual direction, we too need to be aware of divine contemplation as a real possibility for the more generous teens. There is no rule it can't happen to teens. That being said, if a teen gets to this point mentoring should be switched to spiritual direction as he is obviously ready, no matter how young he is physically.

The basis of any holiness is the theological virtues: the air for the soul's lungs. Spiritual life begins from the inside out. Interior life is a union with God that the soul has throughout the day, living in Christ. Through the theological virtues, the Holy Spirit, architect of holiness, dwells in us, and we are "plugged into" throughout the day. It is living in faith, seeing Christ in everything and everyone. It is hoping and trusting in God in daily endeavors; it is loving above all else. A boy, who forms the habit of speaking to Christ and living connected to him while still young, will have strong, deeply rooted spiritual pillars in the future.

Love for Christ is the center of any spiritual growth. Boys need to experience Christ as their best friend so they can respond with a personal, real, passionate, and faithful love. This love should be a driving motor in one's own life of grace, in practicing the Christian virtues and in extending Christ's kingdom. Such love is only real if it is freely given, we cannot force a boy to follow Christ, but as mentors we present his grandeur and his call to the boy.

A logical consequence of loving God is following his will. An important part of the spiritual life is discovering, embracing and following what God wants of an individual in each moment. The first part of God's will is obedience to authorities like parents, teachers, and the police. Beyond this, we need to help form the boys to discover God's will, but we should never impose it.

Mary wants all the boys to be Holy. Never forget this most intimate aid you have. As St Maximilian Kolbe said, "The nearer we come to the Immaculata [Mary], the more we become holy."[11]

The spiritual life is built on a strong foundation of human virtues: first the man, then the saint. God can achieve much more in a soul if he has the human base to build his work upon. Many times in the spiritual life one does not progress because of a lack of human virtue, such as constancy or willpower. This human formation does not make a boy holy on its own, but should team up with each of the other principles: fundamental option, spiritual battle, theological virtues, love for Christ, obedience, and Mary.

Means for Spiritual Growth

To progress spiritually, certain elements are essential. These go together like the sugar, flour, eggs, and chocolate chips in grandma's chocolate chip cookie recipe: pure perfection. They should be applied the same way grandma uses her recipe: not by perfectly measuring out each one, but by putting a lot of love into them all. We have seven ingredients in this recipe.

The first ingredient is prayer: this is not just an action but a constant attitude. One cannot progress in spiritual life if one is not in constant contact with the source of all graces. Prayer changes hearts. One cannot live like Christ if one does not know him or speak with him. One cannot pretend to love God if one does not make time for him every day.

God's grace is what makes the flower grow – it's the second ingredient. One needs the sacramental grace from Reconciliation and the gift of the Eucharist to be able to fight temptations and renew one's decision to be close to Christ. His grace sustains and feeds souls. The sacraments are the visible signs and channels of God's grace. In this aggressive world, the sacraments are essential.

"In our present state of fallen nature, it is *impossible* for us to love God truly and effectively without sacrificing ourselves for Him."[12] Jesus said that unless a grain of wheat falls to the earth and dies, it will not bear fruit.[13] Christ chose the cross and suffering to save mankind. If one wants to grow spiritually the third ingredient is denying oneself so as to opt for him and do what shows more love for God and less love for oneself. "Perfection consists essentially in the love of God and of the neighbor carried unto sacrifice."[14] One can fake surrender for a while but if it is false, eventually it will be revealed.

Love is self-giving. If one is truly trying to be like Christ and progress spiritually one cannot ignore the surrounding world – God is present to those in need. He needs help and hands of his people in his work of salvation. Love for others is the fourth ingredient.

The fifth ingredient is spiritual friendships or fellowship. Any youth ministry should give concrete means to progress spiritually: prayer time, retreats and service projects. The activities of a youth group also provide friendships and fellowship that exert positive peer-pressure. Youth ministry presents the ideal, Christ, in a way appropriate to the boy at this moment.

The sixth ingredient is a personal commitment to follow Christ. Boys are not yet as stable as adults but a personal commitment to Christ can solidify their work. Certain programs, such as ECyD, also offer a way that the boy can commit to a closer following of Christ by promising personal prayer, virtue, and friendship with Christ in addition to participation in the activities.

Mentoring – the final ingredient – is the concrete moment set aside to focus on how one is doing spiritually. This time of reflection, formation and listening to the Holy Spirit is a beneficial means in the life of any Christian. Mentoring should be the means that brings everything else together and makes it personal. Here we propose the principles and encourage the boys along the means. It should be the moment when all the other ingredients come together.

With all these ingredients we can prepare teens for a solid spiritual life. Not only will it be sweet like cookies but it will give them the energy to progress through the various stages of the spiritual life.

12. TEENAGE SPIRITUAL PRINCIPLES

Dominic listened attentively to the talk. The priest finished. Praying a little while, he remained in the chapel alone. For the next few days, he said nothing, going about very quietly without his usual joyful spirit. His companions noticed this, and so did the priest. Thinking something was wrong, the priest called Dominic aside,

"Is something wrong?"

"No," Dominic said, "something is right."

"What do you mean?"

"I feel that I must become a saint. I never saw before that it was both possible and easy. Now that I see it, I can have no peace inside until I really begin to do so. Please, will you help me?"

"That's good, Dominic." The priest said, but added that he should not get worked up, stay cheerful, and continue his regular life of study, games, and piety.

Both those involved in dialogue are now saints Canonized by the Church, St John Bosco and St Dominic Savio, who remains the youngest non-martyr canonized. From this talk, Dominic Savio made three resolutions that can serve any boy up to the present day:

1. That it is God's will that each one should become a saint.
2. That it is easy to become a saint.
3. That there is a great reward waiting in heaven for those who try to become saints.[1]

Sainthood is what we are seeking in each boy. It is the spiritual principle of principles for anyone. However, we need to make it a little more concrete at times.

This chapter provides a brief overview of some convictions, loves, and virtues that are extremely helpful to grow spiritually during the teenage years. These should provide the bedrock upon which specific programs can be developed for groups or individual teenagers. A conviction is a belief that is deeply rooted in the soul to the point that it becomes unalterable in the boy's mind. The "loves" here are those things which motivate a boy. If a boy loves a girl who is a violinist, he enjoys listening to her play. If a boy loves souls, he will come to enjoy apostolate. Finally, 10 key teen virtues are listed.

Five Convictions for Teens

Not everyone has serious convictions, but everyone who changes this world does. Even those who have done immense evil have had deep convictions that drove them. Hitler really believed what he said. Obviously, we need to plant convictions in the boys that will drive them on towards good not evil. In fact we want to drive them towards the best, not simply the good.

These convictions summarize in many ways what we want to help the boys become. They need to be behind all we say in mentoring and in every boy's mind. Meditate on them so you can communicate them and teach boys to do the same.

God Loves Me: God my Father created me to be with him in heaven and sent his Son to redeem me by pouring out every last drop of his blood. Christ is my brother and best friend who comes to me in the Eucharist. I often conclude my e-mails with "Jesus loves you!" to emphasize this conviction. This conviction transforms boys. God's love is the one thing that doesn't change in a world changing more quickly each day. If they realize this, they will not be searching for love in inappropriate things. This is the first answer to the deepest questions they begin to ask: "Why am I here on earth? Who I am? Is there meaning in this life?"

God's Will: If God exists and he loves me and he created me, then he knows what is best for me and what will make me happy. So, God's will is the most important thing in life to discover and to do. Adherence to God's love flows directly from awareness of his love. A boy needs to hold onto it firmly, even when it is difficult.

My Happiness and Holiness: Jesus calls us to himself. He calls teens too. A boy needs to be convinced that the ultimate fulfillment in this life is found in God, in becoming holy as God has called him to be. Holiness is not corporate but personal. It is not the call of a telemarketer but of a friend and father. God calls each boy to a particular model of holiness just like he called, St Peter, St John, St Paul, St Francis, St Ignatius Loyola, St John Bosco, Bl. John Paul II, Ven. Fulton J. Sheen, and a whole army of other saints to follow him in a unique way. Mentoring should light a lamp so that a boy can see the path he needs to follow.

My Mission: Following on God's call to be holy and happy, God calls each of us to a certain mission. God calls each to work in the vineyard, but some will plant and others will reap. Boys need to realize the transcendental importance of their mission – souls depend on their fidelity – and hence be driven to work hard. If we love others, we will want to bring Christ to them.

My Priorities: Following from God's call to holiness, happiness, and spreading the kingdom, each boy should be able to set his life on the straight and narrow path with the priorities of the Gospel. A boy who has understood the first four will see the need to prioritize his daily prayer time over 10 more minutes of YouTube. This conviction builds his daily life around the other four. This practical element of priorities makes this conviction the hardest. How much we would like to spend a few more minutes on Facebook when we know we should do something else.

These five convictions give teens a spiritual foundation in God's love. They begin with his love and move to its practical effects in this boy's life. If we want to transmit them, we first need to take on the challenge of living them.

Five Things Every Teen Should Love

Without love we are like a Ferrari without a motor. It looks nice on the outside, but it won't go anywhere. It may attract people, but when they get inside they will realize there is something missing. St. Paul said, "Without love I am nothing. And though I give away all I own to the poor and offer my body to be burned, and have not love, I do not gain a thing."[2] Love is the motor that moves a person.

God's love was the center of the five convictions. Now we move from the love God has for teens to what they should love in response.

Love is not girly – even though they talk about it more – but the decision that a good is more important than oneself. To love is to will the good of the other above one's own good. Love is persevering through time, not momentary, because if good will is only for a minute, it inevitably lets the other down – which amounts to the opposite of love. Mother Teresa was a perfect example because she wanted the good of the lepers in India above her safety, comfort, and health. A mom who stays up at night with a sick child shows her love. Someone who donates from their surplus but nothing more loves poorly because they will the good of the other, but not above their own good. As persons, it is only proper to love persons. We might say, "I love pizza," but we only mean that pizza is very pleasing to us. We can't "love" it according to this definition.

Love for Jesus: Boys need to learn to love Christ as a person; if he remains abstract the boys cannot love him. Love implies being faithful, not a flash in the pan. If this love is constant, it will become passionate because Jesus is love itself.

A mentor needs to remind the boy: "Try to do *all* for love of Jesus; he is so good that he accepts the least thing, provided that it is done out of love."[3]

Love means Jesus takes first place in the teen's heart. He is the first love because he has loved first, as we mentioned above. There is nothing more real in this world than Christ's love, so he deserves real love in response. We need to lead the boy to a profound experience of Christ's love so they want to respond by loving him. His love can be found in the Cross, the Gospels, and the Eucharist.

Teens need to love Christ internally and externally. Internally, love is shown through the life of sanctifying grace and deep prayer, communicating with their best friend. Externally, the boy should witness Christ's love through personal example and spreading faith in Christ. Offer them concrete ways to make their love real.

Love for Mary: Mary is the mother of each boy. A tender filial love should drive a boy to become like her, to imitate her virtues like faith, piety, humility, and generosity.

Christ loved his mother immensely. If we want to imitate him we should love Mary immensely too. She understood Christ better than anyone else ever can; she was the one God chose to bring Christ into the world. Be grateful for her "yes" to God's plan of salvation. Christ gives her to us as our mother under the cross, "Behold your mother,"[4] so boys need be faithful sons. They must see Mary's example and how imitating her virtues pleases her. Everything can be entrusted to her. She wants to be part of these boys' lives.

Love for the Church and Pope: The Church is both Christ's mystical body and his bride; if one loves Christ, one will love the Church. The Pope is the man God has chosen to lead the Church. He is the Vicar of Christ; he is my shepherd with 1.2 billion of sheep to watch over. The Pope loves every single member of his flock. All Catholics are united through the Church through the Eucharist. The Church suffers throughout the world and the teens need to fell her suffering.

To love the Church, the first step is the awareness that they

FR MATTHEW P. SCHNEIDER, LC

are part of this Church. Boys live love for the Church every time they chose holiness in daily life; virtue, prayer, and all true Christian life necessarily include love for the Church because the Church needs authentic apostles who love Christ. Teens need to understand what the Pope and the Church teach. Memorization of doctrine may work at 11 or 12, but soon it doesn't suffice; they need to understand his teaching so they can defend him. Obedience to all the Church and Pope teaches also shows love.

This love should extend beyond just the Pope to the local bishop, even to the parish priest or school chaplain. The Church is present in every member, but her sacred ministers manifest her in a special way.[5]

Love for the Souls: Jesus came, suffered and died to save souls. So many of them now live in confusion and are so far from this salvific balm that our Lord provides. All Catholics, by baptism, are responsible for bringing the message of Christ to souls. We cannot save a soul – only Christ can! Instead this love is expressed by bringing souls in contact with Christ through apostolates (in contact with his word, with his presence in the tabernacle, or his charity through the boys hands) and by prayer asking Jesus to not let any souls fall into hell.

Love for Family and Friends: All of these other loves would be useless, if the boy doesn't love those closest. St John says, "If anyone says, 'I love God,' and hates his brother, he is a liar; for he who does not love his brother whom he has seen cannot love God whom he has not seen."[6] Boys need to seek to serve and be generous in the practical everyday life – loving means putting others before oneself. When mom asks to take out the trash, the boy stops and does it right away; when he has 2 candies, he shares one with a friend; and instead of insulting his sister, he compliments her.

Ten Virtues for Teens

These ten virtues are important for teens to live in everyday life. When a teen lives one of them, he will notice that the others improve as well because all Christian virtue is united. If one works on faith, that implies also working on obedience because faith is adherence to what God revealed. The next 2 chapters are dedicated to prayer so it isn't here explicitly but is implicit in a few virtues. **Charity** is the love of Christ brought into our love for others. A charitable teen is kind, respectful, courteous, and helpful to all. He forgives others easily, and always helps those in need: spiritually, morally, and materially.

Faith means accepting God and all that he communicates through the Church and his own conscience. What we know by faith is what we know best, better even than what we see. Faith also drives a boy to pass on the truth of Christ to all.

Purity is one of the most delicate virtues. Boys are discovering themselves in this area. They become aware: "Masculinity-femininity – that is, sex – is the original sign of creative donation and at the same time the sign of the gift that man, male-female, becomes aware of as a gift lived so to speak in an original way."[7] At this volatile time of discovery temptations against purity can be very strong. We need to lead boys in the *direction* of chastity, not just keep them from the *line* of impurity, as was described in Chapter 7.

Humility comes by recognizing that one is a needy creature who has received everything from God. It is perfected when this littleness is put at the service of others and the boy seeks to improve himself. Humility is the basis of self-knowledge and hence "is truth".[8]

Responsibility includes trustworthiness, fidelity, and the ability to get it done. Children are rarely responsible but all successful adults need to be.

Honesty is not just to avoid lying. Honesty makes no truce with sin (for example: I'll watch this bikini-clad babe but I'm still pure). Mediocrity is opposed to honesty because the boy knows what Christ has called him to.

Generosity means giving oneself to God and others without reserve. A generous person gives not only of things or extras, but of his time and himself; even to the point of sacrifice in imitation of Christ on Calvary.

Tenacity means fighting to the end and not giving up, like a soldier. In prayer, in charity, in apostolic service, it is easy to get worn out and tired, but boys need to learn to fight to the end. If they can fight now when they have natural tiredness from growth, they will be able when they are adults.

Obedience is not feeble submission, but loving trust in and respect for God, the Church, parents, teachers, and leaders in their youth club. It should not stifle the boy but lead him to fullness.

Joy may seem odd here. It is essential. One of the biggest lies today is that a spiritual life, holiness, is boring. If a boy is sad, is Christ really in his heart? Christ is the best friend a boy can have and should lead him to a contagious joy.

The center of teenage spiritual principle is God's love. From God's love, four other convictions flow forth. As a response to these convictions, the teen has certain things he needs to love: Christ, Mary, the Church, Souls and those close to him. This convictions and loves are manifested in ten general virtues which are made specific in the concrete circumstances of each teen.

13. PRAYER

What is prayer? Through prayer, the soul breathes. No one can build a deep friendship without communication and time together; likewise with our spiritual life, our friendship with Jesus Christ. St Paul urges us: "Pray without ceasing."[1] Christ himself admonishes us: "Watch and pray that you may not undergo the test. The spirit is willing but the flesh is weak."[2] Blessed Charles de Foucauld said, "To pray is to be with God."[3] Prayer is communicating with God in faith and friendship. The *Catechism* gives 3 general definitions of prayer:

> 1. Prayer is the raising of our mind and heart to God, or the requesting of good things from God.[4]

> 2. "Great is the mystery of the faith!" This mystery, then, requires that the faithful believe in it, that they celebrate it, and that they live from it in a vital and personal relationship with the living and true God. This relationship is prayer.[5]

> 3. Contemplative prayer in my opinion is nothing else than a close sharing between friends; it means taking time frequently to be alone with him who we know loves us.[6]

This plethora of definitions might seem overwhelming. Prayer however goes beyond any one definition. Each definition emphasizes a certain aspect of prayer. Depending on your personality and that of the boy you are mentoring, one or another may be the best to explain to him. Teen prayer is not different from adult prayer – just simpler. The content of the conversation changes over the years, as it would do as time progresses in any human relationship, but it is no less important a young age. One learns to pray by praying. The most important factor in a life of prayer is the decision to make prayer an integral part of life. If God matters, one will make time for prayer.

Prayer is speaking, but more importantly it is listening. In prayer we speak with him, we ask forgiveness, we ask favors, we thank him, we adore him, and we praise him – in all this, we await his response. Prayer can use spontaneous or set words. This is a long list of different types of prayer but there are two principle divisions.

First we have public prayer and private prayer. Christ told us "where two or three are gathered in my name, there am I in the midst of them."[7] But he also told us, "when you pray, go into your room and shut the door and pray to your Father who is in secret; and your Father who sees in secret will reward you."[8] Both are good and necessary in a Christian's life. The big temptation at public prayer is to make a show like the Pharisees or be distracted by others.

The other distinction is mental or vocal prayer. All real prayer is mental (internal) or it is not prayer, vocal prayer refers, however, to set prayers that we say like the Rosary or the Our Father, while mental prayer refers to prayer that is a spontaneous dialogue. At the beginning boys need help uniting their heart to the meaning of words already written by someone else in vocal prayer. Usually teens progress from vocal prayer to mental prayer during their teen years. These two types will be discussed in these two chapters.

In the next chapter we will approach different types of prayer, but first we need to know why we should pray. In mentoring, often the *why* is more important than the *how*. We need to convince the boy *why* to pray: he knows intuitively *how* to do it. The *why* is divided into two parts: responses you can give to their inevitable excuses, and what prayer does for them.

Typical excuses for not praying

In mentoring you will encounter the following excuses. I only give one version of each excuse, but teens will often word them differently or indicate their issue in a roundabout manner. To respond well, you need to understand where the error is in each one. At the same time, let him explain their excuse before you respond – even though you know the answer, repeating a response as fast as a computer won't help him out.

"I do not have time to pray." This makes no sense, since "the best used hour of our lives is that in which we love Jesus most,"[9] and this means prayer. St. Theresa said: "The person who is fully determined to make a half hour's mental prayer every morning, cost what it may, has already traveled half his journey." [10] Prayer orients the rest of our life and makes us much more effective. Christ led a very busy life – especially during his public ministry – and yet he made time to pray. We do things we think are important. Boys need to know that prayer is important so it becomes a priority. There is always time to pray because prayer is the principle of the rest of life.

"I don't know how to pray." He is our Father; he will be delight with whatever we offer because *we* offer it. A true father is a lover, not a critic and judge. When his kids mess up, he shows them the right way. Prayer is speaking with someone you love and loves you; he knows you well. He wants you as you are, not an idealized version of yourself. He wants to hear about the little and the great, the good the bad, and the beautiful and ugly of each day. "Look at the incredible ease of prayer. Every time, place and posture is fitting, for there is no time place, or posture in and by which we cannot reverently confess the presence of God. Talent is not needed. Eloquence is out of place. Dignity is no recommendation. Our want is elegance enough; our misery is recommendation enough."[11] The more we do it, the more natural it becomes.

"Nothing happens when I pray." Mentors need to help boys see that prayer is not wasted time, but the best investment of their time. "Prayer is one of the great means to salvation,"[12] and that is the pearl of great price worth giving our lives for. There is so much good going on in prayer that the one praying cannot possibly know it all; only in heaven will we know what graces were given due to our prayer. If a boy has this difficulty, a good question for you to ask is "what do you think should happen during prayer?" From here you can remove this excuse.

"I get along fine without prayer" or **"I am a spiritual person, but I don't pray."** This indicates pride and a self-sufficient attitude. The reality is that "prayer is the *normal*, the *efficacious*, and the *universal* means through which God wills that we obtain all actual graces."[13] (Actual graces are all graces minus our habitual sanctifying grace if we are free from mortal sin.) You need to help the boys realize they need God; being a "spiritual person" without him is a farce. If Christ is the boy's best friend, the least he can do is spend some time with him every day. To get the boy to this point, he needs to see Christ as is friend.

Fruits of Prayer

Christians need to pray because they need God. You cannot transmit what you do not have; to bring others to Christ you must be with him. Let's enumerate four primary fruits of prayer.

First, prayer strengthens us. God asks hard things at times, but never anything we can't do with his grace. He wants boys to turn to him in prayer and ask for strength, to realize that nothing is impossible for God. This is a particularly important lesson during the adolescent years.

Second, prayer orders our priorities. (Remember the 5th

conviction.) Sometimes people develop a warped vision of what is important. Prayer lifts our eyes to the eternal truths beyond the hustle and bustle of our lives. Boys must learn to stop and reflect on what is important in life during prayer, so they can act accordingly. Therefore it makes us a better person. Just as an old married couple start to resemble each other, we will start to resemble Jesus if we spend time with him.

Third, prayer offers consolation. God is the source of true consolation. The devil only tries to imitate God's consolation at deeper levels of prayer. If you have any boy at those levels, he is beyond mentoring – this is where spiritual direction needs to kick in. But consolation doesn't always come, and it is hard for boys when they don't "feel" it anymore; prayer is not feelings. Sometimes we are closer to God when we don't "feel" him than when we do. This lack of feeling can be called desolation. "God generally bestows sensible consolations on beginners in order to draw them to his service; he then deprives them of these in order to test and strengthen their virtue."[14] For example, when a little boy has a friend he gives candy to build the friendship. Over time, the friendship doesn't need the "candy-bond" anymore. However, if it is based on candy alone, withholding candy destroys the friendship – indicating how weak the friendship was in the first place. This happens in prayer. With or without "good feelings," there needs to be a consolation deeper than feelings that comes from those moments with God, the conviction of his friendship and fidelity. God heard him even if he did not hear or feel God; his presence is not dependent on feelings.

Finally, prayer unites us with God and leads us to heaven. All the other fruits come from this fruit. This is the center of what teens should expect from prayer. They may not start thinking about this fruit, but without it, the other fruits will only keep them going so long.

Teens often don't want to pray but prayer is essential for any spiritual growth. You need to be equipped to respond to their excuses and explain the fruits they will receive. Once they begin, these lessons on prayer are needed to strengthen their desire to pray.

14. Specific Types of Prayer

"So how are you doing with your commitment to reflect five minutes on the Gospel each day?"

"Well, I do it – at least most days. But, I mean, I never really seem to learn much. I read one chapter and nothing comes."

"OK, how do you read it?"

"I mean, I open up and read."

"Just like you would read a novel your English teacher gave you?"

"Yah, I guess, more or less."

"Well, is the Bible just like any old novel?" His head shakes. "So maybe you should read it a little differently."

"But how?"

"Try reading it paragraph by paragraph, slowly and thoughtfully, and reflect and pray after reading each paragraph. Be simple about it, and just ask Our Lord during each reflection, 'Lord, what do you want to share with me in this passage?' If you don't get a special light, just keep reading. If today no special insight comes, don't worry. You have prayed and spoken with Jesus, listening to his word."

"OK, is that all?"

"Two more things: if you receive a special light, stay there, and pray about it to discover what God is trying to tell you; and remember St. Jerome says that 'ignorance of Scripture is ignorance of Christ'."

"OK, I'll try that."

A few weeks later, the boy came up to his mentor, and said that he had read Luke 15, and when he read the passage where Jesus says that there is greater rejoicing in heaven over one repentant sinner than over 99 righteous people, he received a special light, discovering that he really mattered to God; that God's love was personal, and that he was waiting for him in heaven.

This is but one example of how prayer causes spiritual growth. Willing to pray is not enough. To actually pray you need to pray some *type* of prayer. Today, it seems like every month some new secret-formula prayer is invented: centering prayer, Reiki, labyrinths, or whatever other method. I don't know too much about most of these; I tried walking a labyrinth once and didn't help me too much. It seems some are more psychological and some others seem contrary to Christian truths.[1] Instead of trying this or that new-fangled prayer method, I have stuck to the prayer methods that have been effective through 2000 years of Church history. Obviously, such methods need to be adapted slightly for the teens of today but their essence remains intact.

Each type should lead to the others, but they are each a different type. Teenagers begin with the sacraments. Add on vocal prayer. Vocal prayer should slowly transform itself into mental prayer. Sacraments are the most important form since they are "efficacious signs of grace."[2] Mental prayer is next as it is direct contact with God. Vocal prayer, however, is essential at the beginning to lead the boys to the other two.

Sacraments

Except for one year (Confirmation) or a serious illness, the only sacraments most boys will receive as teens are the

Eucharist and reconciliation. These two can and should be repeated often and are important for driving the boys' formation in all areas.

As Catholics, we are all obliged to attend Sunday mass. Your teens should not just *go* to mass; they should live mass with the right attitude and dispositions: with respect, attention and recollection. They need to see the miraculous gift of the Eucharist and the importance of God's word so that Sunday Mass does not become routine. His whole Sunday should be ordered to the moment he receives Jesus. If he goes to a Catholic school with weekly mass or has another opportunity throughout the week, encourage him (but don't force or insist, as such tactics can often backfire a few years down the road; I've seen a few cases).

Sometimes boys seem bored because they don't understand mass. One author invites everyone to put 3-D glasses of faith to see what is happening in the Mass. If not, so much is missed! Following with a Missal[3] in hand and reading along helps to understand the Mass. The key moment of Mass for teens should be receiving communion so that Christ lives in them. Encourage teens to take time (5 minutes or so) after receiving communion to give thanks to God for the gift of the Eucharist. Bl. Columba Marmion speaks of how Communion builds docility and it builds other virtues similarly:

> I cannot conceive how a person who received Our Lord in Holy Communion, and to whom he has given all, even his Precious Blood, can say afterwards, "I know that would give pleasure to Our Lord, but I will not do it."[4]

Another question is avoiding sacrilegious communions. Boys should try to receive Jesus in the Eucharist as often as possible since it is the grace of graces in this world. However, if they have an unconfessed moral sin on their soul, they need to go to reconciliation first. We need to encourage boys to be honest about this.

That brings us to the sacrament of reconciliation, the

ordinary means to eliminate mortal sins after baptism. This sacrament is not just for mortal sins but to help boys grow in grace by eliminating even small venial sins from their soul. Many boys are hesitant about going, even if they understand the sacrament. If they are uncomfortable to go to-face-up with a priest they know and confess one's sins, suggest that they use the screen. Just because it makes a boy uncomfortable does not diminish its importance. Reconciliation is an encounter with Christ. "In this sacrament each person can experience mercy in a unique way, that is, the love which is more powerful than sin."[5] God knows us and our heart perfectly already. In reconciliation, we ask forgiveness for our faults *to Jesus* through the priest. Boys may be more willing if they know Jesus is waiting for them. The priest is the instrument that God chooses and it doesn't matter which one. Small guides to prepare a good reconciliation can help too.

We need to encourage frequent reconciliation. I don't think a magic formula exists here. Two weeks is an excellent frequency if available. Once a month also works. Once every three months – "the oil-change method" – is a minimum if we are trying to help this boy grow in holiness. Remember Mother Teresa went every week.

> What often blocks the action of God's grace in our lives is less our sins and failings, than our failure to accept our own weakness – all those rejections, conscious or not, of what we really are or of our real situation. To 'set grace free' in our lives, and paving the way for deep and spectacular changes, it sometimes would be enough to say simply 'yes' – a 'yes' inspired by trust in God to aspects of our lives we've been rejecting.[6]

These two sacraments – the Eucharist and reconciliation – are the center of prayer but beyond prayer. We encounter Jesus as a real person each time we receive a sacrament.

Vocal Prayers

Vocal prayers indicate prayers that are pre-formulated: the Our Father, a short morning prayer, a decade of the rosary, or the Divine Mercy chaplet for example. For these prayers, boys need help on various levels.

The first step is remembering to do them. Boys should commit to some daily vocal prayer, something as simple as an Our Father and Hail Mary every morning and evening. However, boys are not the best at remembering such things so we need to help them. As mentors, we need to find a way that they make it part of their daily routine. A few suggestions might be: placing a prayer card on the nightstand, taping it to their mirror, or having them always get out of bed, kneel down, and say morning prayers before they do anything else. It is typical that boys are tired at the end of the day and they can't think of anything beyond the pillow, so night prayers can present an added difficulty. You may want to help them learn to get to bed at a reasonable hour so they are not absolutely wiped; as well, there is no rule that night prayers have to be after *everything else*, so the early evening will work when they are occasionally up late.

The second step is helping them to not just repeat the words, but make it a prayer from their heart, to make it a mental prayer as well as a vocal prayer. They need to remember who they are speaking with – Jesus, God the Father, or Mary – and what they are really saying. Most common vocal prayers have an incredible depth of words that is lost by "heymaryfullagracedalord's…" Oftentimes, spending 10 seconds in silence to put oneself in the presence of God is a good beginning. Another help is very often having a small holy card, statue, or crucifix to fix the imagination on. Changing this image occasionally adds freshness during the teen years.

Some vocal prayers, such as the Rosary, are specifically designed to lead towards mental prayer. As a boy prays a decade of the rosary, he can either reflect on the mystery or on the precise words of the Hail Mary, but either way leads towards mental prayer.

Mental Prayer

Mental prayer indicates any prayer that is not a set formula but something a boy improvises himself – it is a dialogue with Jesus. Mental prayer ranges from reading about a saint or making a 5 second petition to a weekend retreat with other boys. Teens need to be introduced slowly to different forms of mental prayer. As a teenager, he finally possesses a level of mental reflexivity that he can go deep in mental prayer. He is not yet fully burdened by adult responsibilities like a wife, kids, and a job, so this is the ideal time to develop a habit of mental prayer. Let's examine 5 areas of mental prayer: good reading such as lives of the saints, spontaneous prayers, visits to the Eucharist, conscience exams, and reflections on the Gospel or meditations.

Teens need to see Christ progressively as a leader, a guide, a friend, and an apostle. The lives of the saints provide examples of Christ as each of these. They present a hero who had Christ close rather than one who is the best at a certain sport or conquered others. It is good to know a few books in this category beforehand so you can suggest them to boys. You can also find many lives of the saints in the Catholic Encyclopedia which is free online (at Catholic.com and NewAdvent.org). Catholic.net also has a daily saint on the front page. Daily contact with such examples helps boys organize their lives around the ideals of the saints not the latest pop star. Once a boy is ready, good books like this help him go deep. For example, it would be a good idea to keep a sheet of paper in the book and write down lights as they read. For younger teens, the Bible and lives of the Saints are usually the best spiritual reading to do; as they get older some adult spiritual books can be added in the mix. Unfortunately there are few systematic books written for teens that challenge them with a maximum spiritual life, not a minimum.

Throughout the day, there are many opportunities to say

short spontaneous prayers to unite ourselves with God. As a boy walks between classes he can say a quick one line prayer to remind him that Jesus, his best friend, is near. Sometimes these are petitions, such as "Jesus, help me understand Chemistry" or "Mary, watch over that poor beggar on the street." Sometimes it is thanksgiving, "Thank you for this beautiful sunset." Sometimes it is just presence, "Jesus I want to be with you." The Church has developed several short prayers that are often helpful to use at such moments which you can teach the boys in a few seconds. One is the Divine Mercy Prayer: "For the sake of his sorrowful Passion, have mercy on us and on the whole world." Another is the Jesus Prayer or Prayer of the Heart which Russian monks repeat hundreds of times a day: "Lord Jesus Christ, Son of God, have mercy on me, a sinner." A third is the second half of the Hail Mary: "Holy Mary, Mother of God, pray for us sinners now and at the hour of our death, Amen."

As teens get older, say about 14 or 15 years old, it becomes important that they dedicate three to five minutes to simply be with Jesus each day. If the boys have a tabernacle close, it is best spent before it, but if not, just find a quiet corner. In a visit, ideally, boys just speak to Christ, telling him what is most in their hearts. At times they may not know what to say but that is fine too. Just being with your friends sometimes is what is important. Perhaps looking at the cross and speaking to Christ there crucified, talking to him about the Gospel reflection they read about today, or even just telling him their day. A prayer journal can help some teens. If they are still stumped find them a good spiritual book to read and reflect upon in such visits.

As well, once a boy reaches his middle teens, he should begin some kind of daily review which ends with a commitment to do better the next day; this is called a conscience exam. It should be simple – reviewing their rule of life (see chapter 17) or a few questions such as the ones below to help them examine themselves. They can write these questions on a post-it or their iPhone to have them handy.

First of all, what do I have to thank God for today? What have been the signs of his love for me? It helps to go over the day part by part (school, homework, youth group, family dinner, etc.). How have I showed God my love today? Have I remembered him in prayer? Did I fulfill my commitments? *How* did I fulfill my commitments? Have I loved God by loving others today? In my thoughts? Words? Actions? Have I been a good example in everything I have done? Have I tried to bring others closer to Christ?

A Gospel reflection refers to reading a passage of the Gospel and then reflecting; it can also be called *lectio divina*. (*Lectio divina* sometimes implies a more specific method; these specific methods do not go against what is said here and if you know one don't be afraid to teach teens.) This is a prayerful reflection, not intellectual study or apologetics, and should prepare the way to adult meditation. The goal here is to know Christ, and transform our life to be like his. "Scripture is in fact and above all a means for knowing the power of the living God, who reveals himself in it, just as he revealed himself to Moses in the bush."[7] Once a boy commits to this, make sure he finds 5 to 10 minutes to do it in his daily schedule. After he has been doing it a few months if he is 15 or older, he may want to up this to 15 or 20 minutes. Be cautious not to over commit a boy here because after one powerful experience boys often want to go all in, but then when they realize such powerful experiences are few and far between, they get frustrated and give up.

The reflection has various stages. First, the passage is read. Here the boys need to try and see the scene, not just read the words half-distractedly. Next, the boy needs to ponder the passage. What is Jesus trying to tell him today? Third, he should pray as a response, asking for strength to fulfill this resolution Christ asks through this passage. Finally, he contemplates, listening attentively for what God wants to say. At different times and with different boys, the stages can take varying percentages of the time. When boys begin, reading and seeing the scene is often over half the time and they have trouble listening silently more than 15 seconds, but the latter stages tend to absorb more time as they progress. These stages are not a fixed rule but a guideline given the general practice of the Church.

The Gospels are the Word of God, so they speak to boys in their everyday situations. There are two great ways to do Gospel reflections, either pick a Gospel and read it sequentially or get a Missal and read the Gospel from daily mass.

If the boys have trouble, several different pre-made reflections are available. *The Better Part* by Fr John Bartunek has a more in-depth description in the introduction and reflections on the entirety of the four Gospels. *In Conversation with God* by Francis Fernandez also has spiritual reflections on the Gospels (although the complete set is 7 volumes and $150-$200). A final option is to have the boys sign up for free daily meditations at Regnumchristi.org[8] or read a meditation from Catholic.net. Fernandez and both websites base the reflection off the Gospel of the day. There are a few others beyond what I listed and new ones spring up from time to time. Remember, you can't give what you don't have: your personal meditation is most important.

Retreats are often turning-point moments in a teen's life that bring together a whole bunch of these different aspects of prayer. A single weekend retreat can often equal a year's growth in prayer. We need to find Catholic retreats for teens in our area (obviously ones that are orthodox, formative, fun, and insured). As a mentor it is often useful to go to such retreats to mentor the boys at least once.

Each of these types of mental prayer should have a place in a teen's life. What place each has can vary between teens. Some will find more fruit reading while others will find more fruit just silently talking to Jesus in the tabernacle. You need to see with each teen what helps him grow most.

Time Dedicated to Prayer

We need to remember that we are working with teen boys,

not contemplative nuns. They may or may not pray as a family. They may or may not have access to weekday mass. They may have few extra-curricular activities or a stack of them. In other words, each boy is unique.

Obviously, we need to start with the very basics and add on other things progressively. Start with something simple, like praying an Our Father and Hail Mary when they get up and when they go to bed. But once the teenager says those basic prayers, some boys will tend to become too contemplative and we may need to limit the time such boys commit to daily prayer to avoid scruples. We should encourage them to use every minute of prayer well.

Some youth organizations, such as ECyD, give the boys specific prayer commitments when they join. Usually these are well-adapted to the boy's age so you need not add more. If the boy wants to add more, limit them to double what is required; teen boys need to run, serve, and grow.

I would aim for 10-20 minutes a day for younger teens and 20-30 minutes for older ones; I would avoid getting teens to commit to more than double that unless they are discerning a vocation or something similar. You can but need not count family or school prayers in this time. As boys grow intellectually, the amount they want to pray should grow too. A list of progressive resolutions is listed as part Appendix C (99 simple resolutions).

Prayer is the path to union with God and the basis of all the boys' growth in Christian virtue. As mentors, we need to help them grow in prayer so that they will grow in all areas. Growth in prayer does not primarily mean more time at prayer, but a deeper prayer that affects their lives more dramatically.

A primary focus of Spiritual Mentoring needs to be teens' spiritual growth. Certain principles work for all teens but these principles need to be adapted to each one. The main tool will be sacraments and various forms of prayer. However, it must be based on a solid life of virtue and ultimately on God's love for them and their response to that love.

PRACTICAL ASPECTS OF MENTORING

At the end of the first section on mentoring, I promised you we would go in a big circle and then come back. Here we are. We've covered all the theory and now we get down to application. We talk about the content and some practical suggestions in the first two chapters. The chapter on practical suggestions is one of the longest chapters in the book: each subsection is almost a mini-chapter. Then we move to 2 specific areas: the rule of life which is important for deeper mentoring, and generosity leading to vocations.

15. THE CONTENT OF MENTORING

Now that we have gone over all the theory, let's go into the nuts and bolts. These chapters present a practical guide for mentoring. The content of mentoring is mainly the work of the Holy Spirit. But the little bit that depends on the mentor and the teen allow the Holy Spirit work. These are just suggestions but there is no set recipe for successful mentoring sessions.

Since this session is about the normal content, I want to provide you with a normal mentoring session. To a certain extent, there are no "normal" mentoring sessions since you need to respond to each teen; however, this provides a general outline that works well as a start with most. Throughout the book we have had a number of powerful sessions come out, but here are John Doe and I. (The only change I have made is that this will be a briefer than real life.)

"Hey, John, do you want to talk?" I flag him down in the middle of a soccer game.

"Jimmy, I'm going to talk with Br Matthew a minute," he shouts to the other defenseman.

"So you looked real good in the game, I noticed you were being a real team player: staying back in defense and passing the ball to your teammates." (I was watching the game for a bit to see this.)

"Thanks."

"Well, John, are you doing the same at home, because if I remember right your resolution last time was to work on obeying as soon as mom asked you something?"

"Kinda. I think I got better but my mom always seems to ask me to take out the trash right in the middle of a Mario Kart race, she can't seem to wait till the end."

"But you know you can pause it."

"OK."

"Well just think of all those times Jesus was in the middle of preaching and some sick person interrupted, did he wait till the end or did he cure the person right then?"

"I see your point."

"So how is everything else going?" (I assume he doesn't quite have a rule of life yet.)

"I think pretty well. I mean, other than one math test, I haven't had too many problems."

"Good, now are you saying the prayers at morning and at night like we agreed upon?"

"Yes, most of the time I remember an Our Father, a Hail Mary, and a Glory Be"

"And do you just say them or do you mean what you say?"

"Sometimes at night I just say them since I am wiped out."

"OK, that's good. You mean them most of the time." He nods. "Well, what about adding on one little thing? Why don't you pray one decade of the rosary each day? I know you pray it with your family every now and then but on the other days you could pray just one decade on your own."

"Sure, that sounds like a good idea."

"So when will you do it?"

"I think I can do it once I get home from school." I nod affirmatively and we speak briefly about one or two other areas.

You can see in this story that I am dealing with someone 12 or 13 years old, he's a teen not an adult. Teens are learning to deal with the business of life and very rarely do they have mentoring – preparing for or attending – on their priority list. The mentor needs to help them and lead them along the path heavenward with constancy to the point that it becomes their primary goal in life. Even if a teenager is all over the place, it is important for the mentor not to lose sight of the goal. This goal is unique for each soul based on his background and experiences, talents and shortcomings.

Mentoring gives us a unique opportunity to touch the soul. Over half of people who went to a church last week can't remember a significant insight they gained. Only 29% of practicing Catholics interviewed in the same survey said that attending Church affected their life greatly.[1] Part of the problem is that such teachings are directed at everyone. Mentoring offers us a route directly to this individual person, John Doe in the example. Since it is personalized, it should be remembered and should affect the lives of those we mentor.

Most mentoring sessions follow a fairly basic outline, but the first few sessions are particularly important. Mentoring is done much better if it is prepared. So let's review how to prepare for a mentoring session, how the first few sessions should go, what the general outline of a session should be, one option some mentors like, and the final question in each session.

Preparing for Mentoring

Although mentoring is the work of the Holy Spirit, he needs a human instrument. Think of yourself as the assistant artist to God. You do some of the background and rough out the figures so that the master, God, can focus on the composition and faces. He needs an assistant who follows his plan, but this assistant must be free and creative, not just an inanimate brush.

Both you and the boy need to prepare for mentoring, but especially at the beginning, you need to prepare more. The boy just needs to think and pray about what he needs to go over beforehand. As he advances, having a little index card or iPhone note for resolutions and his rule of life can help.

Pray about the teen. Speak with him and ask God what he wants you to say. Thirty seconds beforehand, refresh in your mind and heart everything you know about that person – who he is, what are his spiritual goals and his resolutions, and what was spoken of in the last session.

It helps to have a little book where you can write down specific information about each soul – like a spiritual journal – and write down what their resolutions were and if possible have a copy of their rule of life. This book must be safe: either in code, in abbreviations and kept in your pocket, or kept protected via computer passwords or a safe. Young boys usually forget their resolutions, but can remember if they are reminded. Anyone can lose their rule of life, and some boys' first problem is he never looks at it, so you need to keep it in mind. Some boys appreciate that you remind them, and others don't care. Being a mentor does not mean that God grants you a superhero steel-trap memory. You are human too.

The First Mentoring Sessions

The first thing you need to do is get to know them and their families, without having it seem like an interview. If they don't think that you are giving them personal advice, they will not value it. They will remain like those 71% of Catholics who receive no great effect from attending Church.

The most natural way to do this is usually by telling them straightforward that you would like to get to know them. They usually want to know a little about your background, and this exchange makes it more natural. It is good to know some things before you begin: his *name*, his age, social status, cultural environment, school, and familial practice of religion. Ask him about his family, about his friends, hobbies, interests, etc. Through his reactions and comments, you should be able to gradually get to know his temperament and character, physical and psychological health, intelligence, emotions and maturity; it is often hard for the boys to express this since they do not yet know themselves well. Sometimes this stage is bypassed because you are already a family friend that the boy knows.

Before any real mentoring can happen, you need common ground for the relationship: mentoring is to help him become a true Christian man under the light of the Holy Spirit, but this often needs to be explained to him. Begin by assuring him he is not in trouble, which is likely the only reason he's been called aside before. At the same time, you should present why you are a mentor and how you can help them (you need to be an example for him or he won't believe you).

If need be, give the example of the mountain. Ask the teen what his goal is in life and how he hopes to find it. Usually, you can help them realize that the goal to any human life is to love God and get to heaven. When you ask him how he hopes to do that, usually the answer is a little more complicated. You are like a mountain guide who can help him along this journey. A mentor cannot carry the person up the mountain or force them to walk the path, but they can help them find the right path. That is why the monthly or biweekly fifteen minutes dedicated to mentoring is a checkpoint where we look at the map and the goal, repositioning ourselves.

You may need to repeat what mentoring is not: psychological counseling, a venting session, or a tutorial for religion class. It is about growing in his own personal relationship with Christ. The better you know the person, the better you can help them. If a boy asks you to be his guide, they need to tell you where they are or he can get lost on the way.

When getting to know him, make sure he is in a comfortable environment to speak at ease; that is why we usually walk or play with boys. They are not at ease sitting down or having a scheduled appointment. If he seems to be put off by walking (maybe he's just finished football practice), ask him if he prefers to sit down on the bench or somewhere else that is casual. Stay in view of others but out of their hearing range. If you go in closed room the boy will likely clam up; plus, your lawyer wouldn't recommend it. The best way to get to know a person is to listen and watch, so don't be afraid to be with the club during activities. Listen to the Holy Spirit, too.

There is a linear progression of mentoring over the first sessions.[2] Even though some boys will move along faster or slower, it is a good guide. The first time the mentor must show human and supernatural leadership, explain to him what mentoring is and how he can best use it. This is the best time to get to know them since then all subsequent times it will be clear you are not doing your work in a cookie-cutter fashion but personalized to him. Some boys open up right away, but don't expect it. During the second session you make a basic resolution with him and briefly explain the commitments. By the third time you speak, you should begin to know him well and should make sure he has some regular prayer and service in most cases. If they are fourteen or older, they should also have a concrete rule of life (see chapter 17) as long as they have had a personal experience of Christ. Even for younger boys, you should have some idea of what they need to work on so the resolutions focus on one virtue rather than changing drastically every session. Subsequent sessions are to help them advance along the path to holiness.

A Possible Outline for Content of Mentoring

There are some specific elements that should not be left out of the content of mentoring, even amidst the simplest or more complex outlines. First of all, it should touch on their spiritual life, their moral life and their apostolic life. In a nutshell, how they are getting to know Christ's love, live Christ's love, and transmit Christ's love. Be concrete and practical with the boys. They should have a resolution from the last mentoring session and evaluate it at the beginning of the next to create continuity between sessions.

The goal of having such an outline is to balance between addressing the boy's immediate needs and working on long term goals in his spiritual life. Christ is the point of reference for both. It is never good to dwell on the problems, but rather, bring God into the picture and try to discern what he would want out of the situation and how he would want him to react. In this way, he learns, little by little, to do God's will in the small and the great things.

Do not let this outline become a straightjacket, nor make it into a checklist. It is a few general ideas that should be touched on regularly in mentoring. How much these elements are "scheduled" depends on you, the teen, and your relationship.

It can help the boy to have a copy of the outline of mentoring so he can prepare. However, you should wait until he has advanced beyond basics. Otherwise it will overwhelm him. For the first few sessions, a small note of his resolutions should be sufficient. If you call a boy and he seems to ramble, ask him if he had time to think and prepare. If not, offer him the opportunity of making a visit to Jesus in the Eucharist to think it through while you call the next boy. If you see that he is still lost, help him go over the outline in a natural dialogue. '

""""Think of this outline like cue cards, not a checklist. Focus on the seven main points which I list below. The sub-points are optional. Every mentoring session should include numbers one, two (if he has one), three, and at least one of numbers 4-7 (usually covering more than one of these is too much for one time).

Before listing them, I want to mention two quick tips I use for applying them. First, I generally pick one theme (usually based of 4-7) as the theme I cover with most boys that month; it makes remembering next month that much easier and I notice I perfect the questions. Second, and this one comes with time, learn how to present numbers 4-7 in different ways. For example I might present 6 as "your relationships with others" one month and "duties at school and home" three months later. Different approaches help teens see their situation from different angles.

1) Review of resolutions agreed upon in the previous mentoring session. (You always need to end with a practical resolution – see Appendix C [99 simple

resolutions] for suggestions.)

    a) You need to remember it! It will transmit to him that you care. Forgetting this is second only to forgetting his name.

2) Analysis of the fulfillment of the rule of life if he has one.

3) General situation of the soul: discouragement or enthusiasm, problems encountered recently with family members, friends, school, etc.

4) Personal duties with God:

    a) Friendship expressed through God's presence both in prayer and during the day, and an effort to find God's will in others or his conscience and obey it.

    b) Prayers: specific prayers he has committed to say: such as morning prayers, a decade of the rosary, or a daily Gospel reflection.

    c) Sacramental life: regular confession and weekly participation in the mass with communion. His life of grace.

5) Duties with self:

    a) Self-knowledge that leads to self-improvement.

    b) Sincerity in word and in life.

    c) Formation of the will which leads to responsibility. Does the environment and media rule him or does he rule it?

    d) Growth in generosity: does he give to others of what he has and of himself.

    e) Joyful purity in thoughts, words, and acts.

    f) Formation: is he diligent in studies? Does he know his faith? Is he attentive to the formational material at youth group? Does he try to use his time well?

    g) Economic simplicity: helping out the youth group and the poor, saving for college, etc.

6) Duties with others:

    a) Family: obedience, respect, affection, etc.

    b) At school: respect and appreciation of teachers, etc.

    c) Friends: true friendships with them, choice of friends, their level of influence on him.

d) Others: politeness, courtesy; positive words about others, etc.

e) Apostolate: What does he do to serve others?

7) Duties with Youth Group:

a) Participation beyond just being there: helping out when needed, creating a positive atmosphere, inviting others, attending retreats, etc.

b) Service projects: does he participate? Do they really bring Christ, not just good feelings? Does he promote them?

It's good to have a more complex outline in mind. Usually I don't try to explain the whole thing to teens. Instead I give a shortened outline: 1. What's Happening in your life? 2. Our resolution from last time, 3. A theme (which I rotate and do the same theme with 90% of the kids each month), 4. Resolution (based off 2 and 3), 5. Open forum (whatever he wants to talk about).

Guide Sheets

A way to help with the outline of spiritual mentoring is guide sheets. I personally have not had the right circumstance to use them but several mentors have told me they find them useful. I give them as an option that you need to judge based on your situations and the personalities of the boys you mentor.

The basic idea is that you make a specific questionnaire based on the theme you want to cover (either related to the retreat you are mentoring at or one of themes 4-7 above). Usually these need to be brief with direct questions. For example a question on a guide sheet about prayer on question was "Which one do you believe to be true about your prayers? (1) God hears my prayers and answers them; (2) God hears my prayers, but doesn't always answer them; (3) God doesn't hear my prayers." I include a guide sheet on friendship as Appendix D.

Using them is simple. You give all the boys the opportunity

to fill them out (usually 15 minutes suffices). Then, when you call that boy, have him grab the sheet he filled out and now you have his basic thoughts on that theme which you can now discuss in mentoring.

How to End Each Mentoring Session

Several different mentors and I have realized independently that one of the most important elements is to always end with an open ended question, "Is there anything else you'd like to talk about?" Most of the time, the answer is "no." However, every so often the answer will be "yes." Sometimes a "yes" is just a question such as "How can Atheists be saved?" but often this is deep personal issues like pornography or family problems.

Some boys have opened up on the tenth or fifteenth time; boys who probably would not have opened up otherwise. I even usually tell boys about the third time I talk to them, that this will be my final question every time so they can expect it if they have something that comes up. Many times they withhold difficult problems until they detect that we listen and adapt to their needs. When you ask this question, be prepared to go deep.

16. Practical Suggestions

Mentoring is lived out in practice. What matters in each mentoring session is not the grand theory, but *this* soul's needs. Every soul and every session are so different that rigid models will never work. The main goal of our life is friendship with Christ amidst the concrete circumstances of every day (which vary dramatically from one teen to the next). Mentoring is meant to guide the soul in this friendship.

The six sections of this chapter are in a logical order but they each deal with something different. They are practical suggestions, not rules. They are not all of equal value. First we will speak of your own holiness as the bedrock of any successful mentoring. Next follows teamwork with the others necessary to carry out your mission as mentor. Then I add a few elements that always need to be present in a good mentoring session, which are complimented by a section of concrete suggestions. Working with families, and especially parents comes next. Some legal issues and tough cases round out the chapter.

Personal Holiness

Above all else a mentor must be holy. It is very easy to lose sight of this as one detail among the million things that we have to do each day. However, your holiness is what gets you to heaven and brings all the boys you mentor with you. Holiness is the business of every Christian.[1] And how much more for one who has taken on the ministry of mentoring teenage boys. The devil will set his sights on you, now that you are no longer a simple pew-warmer.

"*Ministry flows from being.* God is concerned with who we are as persons. God first works in us then through us."[2] If we are not worthy instruments, God will have a tough time working through us. This partnership with grace requires both personal prayer and personal study. One who wants to be a good mentor doesn't say once he finishes this book, "now I know all," but, "now I have begun to learn how to be a mentor." There are plenty of books on the spiritual life or on forming teens out there; with the principles of this book, they can be put to effective use as a mentor. I highly encourage you to continue your study of mentoring, but don't go to the extreme. At one point while I was working on this book, I was reading six different books on the spiritual life at once. I joked with my spiritual director that I was having trouble maintaining union with God because of all the books about union with God I was reading.

"The majority of[mentors], even good and virtuous ones, follow in ... their direction of others only reason and good sense, in which a number of them excel. This rule is good, but it does not suffice for Christian perfection."[3] Instead God needs those who are able to hear his voice and obey. Souls who live daily union with him can transmit this to others and lead them to God. Those who follow their own reason only can lead them no further than reason dictates. A mentor needs to be close to God so his voice is clear. This implies personal holiness.

Intercessory Prayer

Since God is the one who will make our mentoring fruitful, why do we so often fail to put it in his hands? All successful ministry is begins, ends, and is sustained with prayer. Prayer helps us put Jesus first, and the teens second so we fade into the background.

This connects directly to holiness as one who is holy will be close to God and depend upon him. Every holy person wants others to be holy. If you want them to be holy, you pray for them. Period.

Frank Mercadante found this secret almost by accident. When he first started, there was no youth ministry so he figured he should pray for each teen in his parish by name so he had something to do (to justify his salary). In his first year, he went from 12 to 120 teens. But that wasn't the highlight for him. Instead, the highlight was that an apostolic spirit was formed where teens lived the Gospel and served like Jesus would.

Since our goal in spiritual mentoring is to go beyond numbers, to discipleship and service, we too need to be praying for each teen we mentor. We need to do so by name. We need to do so regularly, I have a long list but I bring each teen to prayer 4-5 times a week (my list is broken in 3 and I read 2 sections each day in prayer). I don't want to impose a set frequency that you pray for them, but it should be at least twice a week.

If we really want God to enter that teen's life, Mr. Mercadante points out the need to mention what you ask for that teen. "Joe Smithers" is insufficient. We want something along the lines of: "Please help Joe Smithers to really grow in the virtues of humility and patience so can recognize You more." How can we expect the Holy Spirit to build this teen's thirst for him if we don't ask. If we want the best for them, we need to intercede for these teens.[4]

Teamwork

Aiden was fun loving. He made jokes during youth group. He was always the first to participate in sports. He loved his skateboard. Alex had been mentoring him a year and thought he would make a great youth leader.

Mentioning this idea to the other 3 adults who helped out, he got a resounding "No!"

"He comes from a great family but he doesn't have what it takes."

"He listens to his iPod the whole time we are supposed to be learning."

"No, wouldn't Jude, or Matthew, or for that matter almost any other kid his age be better."

Alex was not deterred. He thought they just hadn't seen the wisdom of converting this kid. Alex mentioned the idea to Aiden who loved it. Alex assured him that he would speak with Mr. Jones and that he could start out as a youth leader after Christmas.

Aiden was no different as a youth leader. He disrupted the other youth leader constantly, he passed on his indifference to the boys, and he didn't lead. After two weeks, Alex was at the club and spoke with Aiden, everything seemed to be going dandy and said he liked being a youth leader. Then he spoke with Mr. Jones:

"We have to change that kid, he's worse than before. Sit in the back and see." Alex did so, and saw. He called Aiden over and pointed out 3 points to work on.

"If you don't change, you won't be able to be a youth leader." Aiden didn't change, and three weeks later, he was taken out of this role and never returned to the youth group. A few of the boys lost confidence in the adults directing the youth group. In the end, it is hard to say if Alex had made the right choice but lacked support, or if he erred evaluating this boy. One thing is certain: Alex did not work with his team.

If a mentor works like Rambo, he might help a few kids. But when he works with his team in youth ministry, he can bear much more fruit. Teamwork goes beyond simply existing together; it means working together towards the same goals. This makes your job easier and allows you to help boys more efficaciously. Teamwork has several key elements. Boundary lines are drawn to assign specific roles, but these roles do not conflict with common planning and harmony between team members. Teamwork must be done without breaking confidentiality. Lastly, teamwork should expand from your specific team to the whole Church.

The first thing needed to work as a team is clear boundary lines and respect for the role each one has. Imagine a baseball team where everyone tried to be pitcher. The others need to appreciate your role as a mentor, and you need to appreciate the role of the other leaders who organize or give the group formation. A practical application of this truth is each teenager should have no more than one mentor. If your group has several mentors, divide the boys into groups.

David Murray says: "A professional educator working with kids in a school or youth group environment who does not spend at least thirty percent of every working day dedicated to personal dialogue with the kids has wasted not only thirty percent of his day, but his entire day."[5] I think he has the right idea, but since many of you are dads who have other jobs and volunteer for a youth group a few hours a week, I think specialization is in order. If the team of adults running a youth group does not spend 30% of their combined time in mentoring, they will end up wasting their time. If you have 4 adults, 2 should be dedicated primarily (70-80% of their time) to mentoring.

Teamwork should lead to planning and dialogue. Once you know what everyone else is doing, you can easily make an effective little plan for seeing the boys every month. You can also know which boys have leadership qualities or special difficulties that might warrant keeping a closer watch on them. With such a plan, it is good to meet twice a semester with whoever is the top dog to present the results of the past months and look forward to the next few.

FR MATTHEW P. SCHNEIDER, LC

Roles lead to the next element, a harmonious formation. If the group formation is focusing on sincerity this month, the boys will probably be thinking about that, so it would be good to drop a hook or two about sincerity during mentoring. The other leaders know you are giving personal mentoring so they might share observations they have seen regarding certain boys.

Teamwork also implies confidentially on your part. What is told in confidence can never be mentioned to the other leaders specifically. If two or three kids mention that Joe kicks others as soon as the youth leader turns his back, you could say that "some boys said" or mention that, as my mom would always say, "a little birdie told me…" Another example: if someone in the youth group speaks of being lonely or not having any friends during outings, there is nothing wrong with a mentor suggesting to other boys that they might want to hang out with him when the mentor non-so-unintentionally notices that he is sitting alone during the next outing. This is an observation anyone could have.

Sometimes a mentor may see in mentoring that switching Fred to another team may help because Sam is picking on him. If Fred asks the youth group organizer, nothing will likely happen but you can easily ask. In such a situation, the best thing to do is suggest to the boy that you ask the youth group organizer for the change and see if he agrees. Don't tell the youth group organizer why, but if he doesn't trust your judgment, you both need to ask yourselves why.

Finally, teamwork ought to expand to working in collaboration with the whole Church: in the parish, diocese, country, and world. One spiritual author spoke of spiritual direction, and by extension mentoring as the "Church herself reaching out to an individual in the form of an individual and serving to enlighten, to confirm, to corroborate, and to heal."[6] To be fruitful, any mentoring needs to participate in the mission of the Church "to proclaim and establish the Kingdom of God begun by Jesus Christ among all peoples."[7] Christ has willed that all proclamation of the Gospel and all salvation

144

happen through this one instrument, his bride. Other Christians participate in the Church in an imperfect way, but we are full members as Catholics and participate fully in her when we are in a state of grace. If we go outside the Church's mission, outside her plan, we no longer really help Christ. Many other good things are out there, but none of them have the same saving power as Holy Mother Church.

General Aspects Every Mentoring Session Should Have

Even though each mentoring session is unique, certain aspects should always be present. These aspects are not so much concrete items as we saw in last chapter's outline, but attitudes or dispositions. You must be competent and show your competence, you must adapt to each teen, you must motivate, you must challenge, and you always need to be concrete.

Competence: For fruitful work, the boy needs to know that you have specific knowledge and leadership to guide him on the path to holiness. Spiritual leadership is not automatic but must be won by showing proper respect for the teen. You need to empathize with this person. The boy needs to accept you as his mentor, and he will only do that if you accept him, understand him, and have such leadership.

You were trained to lead boys to holiness, you have walked the path of spiritual life, and you are committed to his spiritual growth. When a person feels that someone believes in him and is committed to help him grow, they have a certain respect for that person. To instill such confidence, give him 110% attention and don't rush or check your e-mails while talking with him

Caring: If you don't care for *this* boy, you'll get nowhere. Teens only care to know after they know you care. As St John Bosco said: "Young people should not only be loved, but should also know that they are loved."[8] This starts with a positive attitude but must go beyond that. When they see you are helping them or when you remember what they said, then they know you care.

However, avoid being overly affectionate with kids: no normal forty year-old guy regularly hugs fourteen year-olds except family members, it just seems creepy (plus it is against the child protection norms issued by basically every American diocese). At the same time, don't be a cold and distant robot. Your role as a guide should be warm but distinct from their buddies.

Adaptation: Unless you speak of his specific needs in a manner adapted to adolescent psychology, you can easily become incomprehensible. You need to grab things that are part of their life – images and symbols – because they think according to known images. Images help them express themselves.

Boys desire to change themselves, but need help focusing for things like the rule of life (see chapter 17). At the beginning, a mentor has to help him – almost like training wheels – but after a certain period of time, a teen should have convictions or experiences that he can say are the pillars of his spiritual life and what keeps him going.

Motivation: Supernatural motivations are the first kind to have when mentoring. A mentor needs to speak clearly, but, at the same time, motivate the teen for whatever demands his spiritual life may imply. For this reason it is important to go deep and get to know what his real motivations are. Be attentive to him to learn these motivations.

As you pick up his reactions, you should personalize the motivation for him: both what motivation you give and for what action. Some boys may love serving in public. Others may wish they could close their door, read and pray.

Challenging: All boys and young men who have done something great have responded to a challenge. Boys love to be challenged if the challenge is appropriate. Remember depth-confidence from chapter 10. A concrete plan of work needs to be drawn up and he needs to be given little resolutions that you follow up on in your biweekly sessions.

The combination of being understanding and challenging is important. We motivate in order to challenge, we never challenge in order to motivate. We need to help the boys fight for their friendship with Christ – it 'isn't easy. One should imitate the heart of Christ, who knew that the greatest law of all was to love and to demand the best of the beloved. So if one cares for someone, one will ask them for the best.

Concrete: Have clear objectives. If you know his precise situation, you should have concrete goals on the long and short term; have a clear idea of where the soul is headed. Set goals with the boy. Appendix C has 99 simple goals to start you out with ideas. Boys need both clear short term and clear long term goals that match their ideal and help them achieve it. Remember to always review the resolutions before the next session. Take time to pray and reflect on each soul before mentoring. Where does God want him to go?

Based on his individual traits, you can project each boy. Maybe you think this boy can lead a team next year or join the core team in two years – work with him so he is ready. Your notion will probably not be perfect, since the boys and the Holy Spirit may tend towards another goal. If you are in Denver and want to get to Boston, but once you reach Chicago you change your destination to New York, you are still going the right direction. Rarely will your idea be so off that once you get to Chicago, the destination will change to Seattle. Beginning with a plan sets you in the right direction. From this projection, you can set goals in each area that you think the boy can achieve.

Each session needs to move beyond discussion to a concrete decision.

Practical Tips

These are suggestions that I have seen work in the field. Most of them I learned from other mentors – often from two or three. They all come from applying the heart of charity each mentor has to the concrete circumstances in the US and

Canada in the early 21st century. We have spent many pages on *who*, *what*, *why*, and *how*. This section covers *where* and *when*. These things vary from mentor to mentor and teen to teen but I want to offer a few concrete ideas.

When: There is no absolute rule for when the best time to see boys is, but since they tend to clam up if you make an appointment, generally the best time is during the activities of the youth group. Pull them out of soccer for ten minutes and then pull a player off the other side for another ten to make it even. You can even take them out of a talk or a team Gospel reflection, as long as you don't repetitively miss the same activity.

Length: There is no set rule for time. The discussion normally should wrap up after a brief period, especially with early teens who don't have deep self-knowledge yet. Two different rules of thumb can be used to estimate how much time is reasonable. The first is the "2-10" rule: double their age and subtract ten to get an approximate amount of time (12 minutes for 11 year olds but 22 minutes for 16 year olds). The other rule is the "i10" rule. We start a dialogue, and once I as mentor have spoken for ten minutes we conclude. The i10 rule usually comes to equal the 2-10 'as older boys generally have more to say on their own. (However the i10 may not work for all mentors due to personal style).

Even with these averages, don't get worried if every so often you go over or wrap up quick. These are averages to give you an idea. When you introduce the rule of life or when the boy has a personal issue, mentoring may go a little longer, but once it hits double the average, it is time to wrap up and set another mentoring session soon after if you still have things to talk about. His attention span is now gone.

The location: It must be open, visible, and public. If you take the boy in a closed room without a window or far away from everyone else, you can make the boy feel uncomfortable and can incur legal issues for yourself. Teenage boys often feel most comfortable and open up best while doing a simple activity like walking side by side or tossing a baseball. Such activity makes it natural, not forced. Generally, I have found that walking beside the court or field, in attached hallways, or in the parking lot works best.

At a school or more formal setting, mentoring can be done in an office but make sure both of you are clearly visible from outside.

Another way suggested to me (which I've never used) is having 2 or 3 adults mentoring each a teen in the same room.

Most youth groups have some policy to avoid 1-on-1 between a minor and an adult behind closed doors. For example, Life Teen calls there's C² which means always have at least 2 adults and 2 teens together.

Parental Permission: It's recommended that you get permission from the parents before mentoring boys. You can use this moment to begin a relationship with the family. If not beforehand, after one or two sessions you need to speak with them. Parents can feel like you are going over their head if you don't speak with them. Many parents don't really care, but this is recommended based on experience with others who want to know more. Rarely will a parent say "no" but they just want to be informed. Some places – certain states, certain dioceses, or certain programs – require written permission to mentor.

"Spiritual Mentoring": Even though I have been using the terms *mentoring* and *spiritual mentoring* throughout this book, I rarely use it with boys. I find the easiest is just to ask if they want to talk for a few minutes without using any specific term. Several names can work: mentoring, spiritual coaching, personal spiritual training, one-on-one formation, personal dialogue, etc. Several other names should to be avoided for unintentional connotations they can have: for example, *counseling* and *therapy* are both psychological terms. *Spiritual direction* works for some due to its closeness to adult spiritual direction; however, personally I would avoid it since it refers to something a little different and can easily be misinterpreted by parents or parish officials.

Not just mentoring: A mentor should not merely be a traveler passing through town; instead he should be present at the various events of the youth group. This way he will get to know the boys in a natural setting; this allows him to segue into mentoring smoothly and see the boys' strengths and weaknesses beyond what is said in mentoring. Do a service project with them, attend a retreat as an adult volunteer, or meet them with their families at parish gatherings.

Sports Teams: I think that mentoring can be easily applied by coaches of boys' sports teams. The coach needs to find a balance between giving the boy specific technical goals– work on your follow-through when shooting – and larger personal goals as we have discussed throughout.

9 and 10 year olds: I have spoken mainly about 11-18 year-old boys. Sometimes, the dynamics of the youth group demand you go a little outside this zone. If for some reason you are mentoring younger boys, it needs to be simpler, less reflection and more creative examples. Make sure it does not turn into a "friendly chat." It should be a moment of spiritual growth, even from the time he is young. These sessions should be brief.

18 and up: Just as for younger boys, a little adaptation is needed for college-aged guys. This adaptation is less than for younger teens as the psychology should have leveled off already. Help them with spiritual growth but lead them towards a spiritual director. (If you can't find a spiritual director, you can often continue with mentoring beyond its normal limits.) Mentoring is meant to help with spiritual growth up to the point that someone is an adult Christian – psychologically and spiritually – but after that it can become a little redundant for the young man. A twenty-something year old who lives in mom's basement, has a part time job, and spends hours online, is still psychologically and spiritually immature, so you can treat him as a high school student.

Post-mentoring: If you are a mentor for the teen years, you often end up being a consultant afterwards. When someone you mentored starts wondering if they should switch majors in college, you are often a natural person they will want to talk it over with. This can be an immense help to them. In fact, I would encourage staying in contact with them into their twenties and leaving them your contact info so they can always call, e-mail, or TXT you. I did not do this at first and realize that I missed several opportunities to help these young men. In fact, a study of college students found that "an additional year of contact with an adult from the high school ministry [during college] could provide critical support during one of the most difficult transitions they will face. In fact, that contact continues to make a difference two years later."[9] Keep up with them on Facebook (don't be afraid, it isn't that hard – if you are super low tech ask one of those going off to college to help you set up an account), send them a birthday note, talk with them for 10 minutes few months when they come home, and maybe even give them a small personal gift.

Working with the Family

Steve had just finished his degree and moved to a new city to work. Someone put him in touch with the president of a youth club there since he had previous mentoring experience. On arriving, he observed and spoke with some of the dads, noting the key boys at this club, the personalities of the boys, etc. He called one aside for mentoring, then another, then a third. The evening seemed to go well. Mr. Gilson, the club president, liked the fact that now he has someone to mentor the boys.

A few weeks later Steve called up Thomas Smithers whom he'd mentored; Mr. Gilson had given him the number. His mom answered the home phone, Steve spoke with her for twenty seconds, and then with Thomas for ten minutes concerning some ideas for the club.

The next day, Mr. Gilson got a call from Mr. Smithers. "Why was this man calling my son aside and talking to him? I am the one who is supposed to teach my son, and I don't want anyone else interfering."

Mr. Gilson responded gently that he would tell Steve not to do one-on-one again with his boys, but stated how appreciative he is of all the help Steve was giving his own son and the other boys in the club. However, he was unable to diffuse the situation.

In the end, Mr. Smithers pulled his three boys out of the club and took five other families with him. Steve learned his lesson of how important it is to work with families. John Paul II explains the parents' role in educating their kids:

> The task of giving education is rooted in the primary vocation of married couples to participate in God's creative activity: by begetting in love and for love a new person who has within himself or herself the vocation to growth and development, parents by that very fact take on the task of helping that person effectively to live a fully human life. [10]

We as mentors are always assistants to the parents in educating their kids. Unless the parents are doing something seriously wrong, like abusing their kids, we need to work with them and support them. "The right and the duty of parents to educate their children are primordial and inalienable."[11] A mentor can never take that away and must always respect the parents even if they think differently. We can never supplant the role proper to parents.

We can assist parents a bit to be good role models for their teens. If we know of good parenting talks, men's conferences, Eucharistic congresses, or the like, we should take the time to invite the parents of those we mentor.

The family is the child's most important formational environment. Even though many teens want to deny it, they love their parents and often trust them more than friends. If their parents are good examples, they model the boy's entire life.

The future of the family, the Church, and the world is in the hands of the young. We as mentors can lead these boys to the path of pure love where they can find happiness and fulfillment. We need to have sincere love and dedication to the boys we mentor, but this should always be expressed in collaboration with his parents.

To explain how to work with parents, I want to suggest a few key principles of a mentor's contact with parents. A mentor should be in more or less regular contact with the parents, but certain moments are indispensable. The key moments are a general introduction, first personal contact, and calling a boy at home. You and they need to be aware of the limits related to confidentiality, perspective, and affection.

Depending on the situation, it is sometimes best to explain mentoring to parents as a group at the beginning of the year, and sometimes it is best to speak with them one at a time. Either way, all the mentors should be introduced to families at the yearly kick-off.

After you have been introduced to the parents on a general level as a mentor, it is important that you should contact the family when you begin mentoring the teen. This can be done with a simple phone call or greeting them as they drop off or pick up their kids; it's good that you speak once face-to-face within the first month. You need to establish confidence with them. You must build certain credibility as a spiritual leader for their child. It is normal for a parent to worry about who is influencing and dealing with their children, so you may need to "prove" that mentoring is beneficial for their child and you are competent to do it. If they don't want you to mentor their son, don't even think about it. This is absolute. In such a case, you may want to ask if it just you or they don't want anyone to mentor their son. (Don't take it personally, nobody pleases everyone.)

To instill confidence in the parents, take time to explain to them the what, when, how and why of mentoring. Parents need to realize that you have their son's good in mind. Develop a positive attitude concerning the youth group leadership so parents trust the whole team. This works both ways: it helps them trust you because they trusted other leaders, and trust other leaders because they trusted you.

This should lead to an initial stage where you get to know the family. In a way you form the whole family by forming one member because the virtue or vice of one helps lead the others in the same direction. As such it is good to know the family personally.

When you call the home, ask for the parent first and have a brief but substantial conversation. If boys give you cell phone numbers to call or TXT, or their social media accounts check with the parents before you contact them via these means. As a general rule, offer parents the option of getting copied on every TXT or Facebook PM. Texting is considered a more intimate form of communication, and a forty year-old who texts teens looks bad if their parents don't know. (I'm active on social media: my Twitter profile ends with "No DMs unless 18+" and I have checked with the parents of everyone under 18 who is a friend on Facebook. These rules may be a little stricter than you want to follow; I just state them as mine.)

Once a reasonable relationship has been established, speak to the parents regularly. Let the boy know that you will be keeping in touch with their parents, but won't share the content of mentoring. If there are specific subjects mentioned in mentoring that you feel his parents need to know, encourage him to tell them.

As a mentor, you should not tell his parents anything he does not wish, save the tough issues we covered at the end of this chapter. In these cases you should inform him that you will tell his parents, but if there is an urgent need go ahead without his knowledge. (This should only be the case of serious danger.) Although it may damage the relationship with him as a mentor; if his soul or life of grace is at stake, it is the greater good. If on the other hand, you become the confidant for family problems, don't spread to the winds what his mom and dad argue about.

Immature boys sometimes ask that you tell their parents things because they are too shy to. This should usually avoided as it takes away an opportunity for him to mature. His parents need to know as well that there are certain things that are between the boy and his mentor and this confidentiality is important.

In mentoring, you will get to know the boy's family through his eyes; remember this is a subjective point of view. Ask questions prudently to find out the situation and environment in which he lives, but keep in mind that it is to help him spiritually and to help him be an apostle at home. You should know the basics about his family; does he live with both parents, how many brothers and sisters are there, what do his parent's do for a living? Make sure his resolutions regarding his family match his concrete circumstances.

As a mentor, you help one member of the family directly, but you indirectly help the whole family. You need to work with the other family members, especially parents. Help parents get involved in your youth ministry. The more the parents can become involved, the better they will understand and share their children's zeal and the better they will normally appreciate your mentoring. Look for opportunities to invite them to take a glance into the activities.

Sticky Faith found that if 5 non-parent adults at Church invested time in a teen's life, he was much more likely to keep his faith.[12] Getting parents involved in the youth group can make them one of those five for the other teens and be role models for their own teens at the same time. The most important contact you can have with the parents is constantly showing them and their son a model of Christian life.

Tough Cases (and Legal Issues)

You need to be prepared for anything. Whatever the boy tells you, don't look stunned, don't panic, and don't jump for the phone (although some require you to make a call after). You need to be ready for a boy to tell you anything. This section deals with those cases you hope you don't encounter. First, I want to prepare you for them. Second, I want to deal with them by type: abuse and habitual serious misbehavior.

A general tip: once a year spend a few minutes visualizing a boy telling you the worst things possible. That way you 'won't be surprised if it actually happens. Imagine a boy comes and tells you: I smoked pot, I got drunk, I did ecstasy, I masturbate, I look at pornography online, I think guys are sexually attractive, I "hooked-up" (impersonal fellatio and cunnilingus), I had sex, my girlfriend is pregnant, an old man exposed himself to the me, I had homosexual sex, I was abused by my own father (a model citizen), I witnessed a rape, I sold drugs, etc. I am sure the first time you read that list it isn't the nicest experience. Fortunately in mentoring you will only hear one thing at a time, and the scariest ones don't happen every day. Even if initially you aren't sure you can remain calm, trust the Holy Spirit and say a brief prayer before doing anything when you hear something like this.

Even good boys fall at times, and we need to be there to help them out. About 100 years ago, three boys were kicked out of three different Christian schools. One started too many fights, one had dirty pictures, and one doodled during math class. These men come down to us in history as Mussolini, Stalin, and Hitler. How different the world might be if they weren't given up as lost cases over these relatively small things.

Some of these cases are beyond what I can offer in this book, but below are methods to refer them to. For all these cases, however, it is important to know three things before you begin: your diocesan child protection policy, a good priest, and a good psychologist / psychotherapist. The first will specify issues regarding reporting and telling parents. The other two will often be needed to help with these cases since they go beyond your capabilities as a mentor. Just because I say don't freak out, doesn't mean you have the solution.

Sexual, Physical, and Psychological Abuse: In many states (and some Canadian provinces) those giving one-on-one religious counseling (where mentoring falls legally) are mandated reporters, and in some states everyone is. That means that if a boy mentions the physical, psychological, or sexual abuse of a minor you must report it; this is a legal obligation. This does not matter if he is the victim, perpetrator, or a third party (often anything more remote than 2nd hand can be dismissed as a rumor). The only cases where you are not legally bound are where the person is no longer a minor (he is telling you about historical abuse), or if the boy mentions that child protective services or the police have intervened for the case mentioned. It is recommended to report cases of abuse even if you are not a mandated reporter.

To report a case, look up your county's *Child Protective Services* (in Canada it's called the *Children's Aid Society*) in the phonebook, and ask to make a confidential report of abuse. Usually it is best to report it within 24 or 48 hours; if there is immediate danger such as domestic violence call within the hour. If there is no immediate danger, you may want to have an adult family member who knows but is not the perpetrator report it first so that the people at Child Protective Services know he or she isn't complicit. Depending on the circumstances, you need to judge if it is best to call Child Protective Services with or without the family's knowledge. Sometimes you can mention to the boy that you will call and report it at certain time tomorrow and say that it might be best if he or his mom (assuming dad is the perpetrator) call first. In rare cases, you can even call the mom directly after speaking to the teen about it.

If the abuse is simply a threat, in some states you still legally have to act. If you 'aren't legally obliged, I would first discern if the threat was real, and if it was, act! My sister the social worker, who I mentioned back in chapter 3, has to report even more than we mentors do: she says she has to report every time a kid says he will be denied food, even if it is pure show on the kid's part. (He doesn't want the Hamburger Helper his mom left him to microwave because she will be out).

In my years of mentoring, I have dealt with only one case in this regard. Obviously, I can't share the details.

Addictions and Serious Sins: If a boy is involved in a lifestyle of serious sin (lack of chastity, theft, drug dealing, etc.), or addiction (pornography, drugs, alcohol, all night video games, etc.), you may want to pass him on to someone with greater moral authority, such as a priest or a man consecrated to God. Some groups, for example my religious community, have norms that less experienced mentors must pass these cases on. Usually it is sufficient to tell the boy that you think he should talk about it with Fr X, and then tell Fr X that this particular boy wants to talk to him without specifying. It is best to ask the parish priest or a priest close to your youth ministry and figure out how he would like to deal with this situation before it arises.

If you stick with the boy, and he is improving, you can maintain confidentiality. If he continues in the lifestyle, you should reconsider. Normally after a month or two without progress, you should insist that he tell his parents or that you inform his parents with his permission. If he is against this idea, you need to weight the option of going against his desires. Obviously confidentially should not be broken lightly; the teen trusts you, and breaching that trust is a very serious act, only to be taken when other options have been exhausted. If he is still a tween or psychologically immature,[13] telling the parents is usually the right path. He is still a child. For older teens it gets more complex because they are sometimes more adults than children. When these behaviors stem from a desire to affirm his adulthood by rebelling against restrictive parents, the situation is that much more delicate. In such a case, if you deem that the best thing to do is to tell the parents – and it often is – you need to help them find some other means for him to express his adulthood: their tendency will often be to tighten the reigns, which will exasperate the delicate situation.

We want to respect the right to privacy and the right to freedom of conscience with one's mentor, but at the same time we cannot consent to allowing grave evil to continue. His parents have trusted that we will lead their son in virtue, and when that s no longer happening, we have to weigh our options to give the best to the teen. When weighing the options, try to be objective and don't fear being disliked by the teen; that may be needed to shake him out of sin'. The array of circumstances that make each case unique prevent me from giving a hard-and-fast rule for older teens. Sometimes it is best to tell, sometimes it is best not to, and sometimes it is best to stop mentoring a teen hardened in sin if his only use for a mentor is to soothe his conscience. If you decide to tell his parents against his will, tell him beforehand so that he has the opportunity to tell first.[14]

Now this chapter is finally coming to an end so I a summary would be in order. The center of any successful mentor is his personal holiness, which draws teens to Christ. Certain attitudes and practices – first of all teamwork – are needed to accompany these teens on their transformation into adult Christians. I offered a few general guidelines for concrete issues that vary a lot between mentors. Finally, a short section dealt with troublesome things you can hear in mentoring. Next up, a great tool of personal formation for teens: the rule of life.

17. Developing a Rule of Life

Simon walked around the school with Mr. Fitz. After going over last session's resolution and turning past the north side of the building towards the soccer field, Mr. Fitz faced Simon,

"You know what. I think you're ready for the next step."

"What's that?"

"You are working well on these little resolutions we make each month, but I think you are now ready for what's called a rule of life." Simon's face tilts ponderously. "I know you think that it's just for your mom and dad, but let me explain how we are going to do it. Basically, we set one main virtue that we want to work on and then one resolution for each area of your life. You have probably noticed that most of our resolutions the last few months have been about charity – with your brother, with Jeff in your class – right?"

"Yeah."

"Well then let's take charity. If in a few months we realize this doesn't work, we'll change it. But for now, let's just stick to this virtue." Simon nods. "Well let's work out charity in different areas: at home, at school, with your youth group, with strangers, and with yourself. What is the most important part of living charity at home?"

"I need to be charitable with Frankie because he is so annoying."

"Nice, but what will you do?"

"I don't know."

"Frankie is only a year younger than you, so he likes to play a lot of the same things. But if I remember a little while back, you said that *you* always like to pick the games: when you want football, it's football, when you want Wii bowling, it's bowling."

"That's really what happens a lot."

"So why don't you let him pick the game you play?"

"Hmm, OK."

"Here's an index card so you can write it down."

Mr. Fitz continued for another fifteen minutes to make a rule of life with Simon when he was in 7th grade. Five months later, it became useless and needed to be changed, but over two or three years, everyone could see that Simon was becoming a real Christian man.

A rule of life can seem like a huge thing, but it tends to be as simple as the boy who writes it. Despite being simple, it can organize and accelerate spiritual growth if applied well.

I will use the term "rule of life" since it seems to be the most common term among spiritual authors, but many others can be used: program of life, reform of life, my goals for the year, spiritual plan, spiritual plan, formation plan, promises to Jesus, blueprint for holiness, action plan, spiritual roadmap, etc. What is important is the concept of a medium-term spiritual plan that directs all of a boy's formation, particularly his spiritual and apostolic formation. It gives the boy direction for about six months to a year.

> The rule of life enables us *to make a better use of our time* ... He that lives *without a rule* inevitably wastes a great deal of time ... [while] The man who holds by a *well-defined rule of life* saves considerable time.[1]

It is important to explain clearly what a rule of life is to both boys and their parents; parents need to be your allies here with younger teens, although with older teens who are already young men, mom or dad may never hear about it. For the parents there should be no secrets; younger boys can be encouraged to show their rule of life to their parents and let them know that this is what they are working on with their mentor.

As teens get older, a rule of life becomes more important. Sometimes younger teens will still lack the basic maturity to do this, and you can hold it off for a bit. You also need to wait until teens have experienced Christ personally. Many of the teens will have done this before we begin but sometimes we'll be mentoring a teen a few months before this really happens. Until a teen has had some personal experience of the good Lord, the ideal will be empty so there will no motor to the rule.

This chapter will deal with the nature of a rule of life, how to make one, formats for anyone from an 11-year old to the Pope, and how to use one once it's done. I give the most importance and length to the section on how to make a rule of life – that is the meat of the chapter.

What Is a Rule of Life

The rule of life means that this teen is now taking his spiritual life personally. It is a concrete plan that he makes with your help to build his spiritual life. It is not some abstract idea but the concrete battle plan this boy lays out for his specific obstacles. It specifies to the circumstances of this boy here and now what's been said in this book. To explain this, let me begin with a few analogies, then move to self-knowledge, and finish with the importance of the rule of life.

In the Gospel, Jesus tells us two parables that apply to the rule of life. If a man is going to build a tower, he first sits down and builds blueprints and calculates the cost. Today he also makes computer renderings and architectural models. Just imagine how much we would laugh at a tower sitting half-completed for almost 20 years. It is like the Ryugyong Hotel in North Korea which sat 16 years as a concrete skeleton with one rusting crane on top. Likewise imagine how fool-hearty we would consider a king who went to battle with a greatly inferior force.[2] The rule of life is the plan, the means, that each one has for building a great spiritual edifice and conquering vices.

A rule of life structures and gives focus to the spiritual life of a boy. In a war, an army does not attack whatever area or group of people they see. They find out about the enemy, develop a strategy, and designate key targets. In our spiritual lives, we need to know the enemies and develop a plan of attack. A great strategy in war is divide and conquer; it is also the first principle of the rule of life. Boys should know what their goal is, heaven, but they need to choose which battles to fight on the way.

The rule of life requires self-knowledge, self-discovery, and this means a lot to an adolescent. By developing a rule of life they begin to realize why they do certain things. After it is developed, it becomes a great way to evaluate spiritual progress. It helps if they examine their conscience daily, which leads the teen to deeper self-knowledge.

It is not necessarily the only way to grow spiritually, but many will reach a plateau without it and begin to backslide. A boy who has thought about and answered the big questions walks away with great satisfaction because he has a plan to give God the best. Obviously, the greatest effect should be in the daily actions specified in the rule of life.

As a mentor, you should make every effort so that each boy you see develops his own rule of life. Sooner is usually better, but wait until you have seen him a few times so you know him well enough for this endeavor. Take the necessary time with each one, as the fruits will be immense. If it takes 2 or 3 mentoring sessions to develop it, don't worry.

Steps for a Rule of Life

There is no set recipe for a rule of life. Sizes and formats vary, but certain ingredients should always be present. The first element is self-knowledge, which comes from self-examination and leads to personal goals; the second is motivation (an ideal and a motto); and the third is concrete means applied to the boy's life. We'll go through these elements as steps and conclude with signs it was written well or not. Each mentor works differently and the development of a rule of life is different for each soul. Other mentors can give ideas, but find your own method rather than copying others precisely. A rule of life for a 14-year-old boy may be developed in a different way two years down the road. You need to call on the help of the Holy Spirit to lead you in drawing out this spiritual map, since he is the Sanctifier.

Self-Examination: If someone thinks he's in China when he's really in Alaska, he will get bad directions to London. You can't take Pepto-Bismol for a sore throat. Self-examination needs to be sincere and concrete.

To begin we must look at eternity; ask the boy what his ultimate goal is. Obviously, it's getting to heaven or sanctity, but each boy needs to specify it for himself. To start a new building you need to know what kind of land you have and what resources you have. The boy must ask himself *What sort of person am I? What is my goal in life?* Boys don't always intuit the answer so you need to help. Another way to approach it is to ask them to imagine they were 75 and on their deathbed; what would value most?

After they have their goal set, what is the dominant passion that prevents them from achieving it? These can be reduced to three ways to love or trust something else more than God: Sensuality is placing your trust in things, vanity is placing it in others, and pride is placing it in yourself. As time goes on, you may want to specify it a little more for the boys you work with; not pride but self-sufficiency, arrogance, lack of charity, carelessness, or some other species of pride. "Many routes can be taken to find the dominant passion or root vice, and some manifestations in his life. Don't dwell on the self-examination results being negative; instead present them as the first step forward. Thomas à Kempis tells us: "If each year should see one fault rooted out from us, we should go quickly on to perfection."[3] Help them to see it is actually a step forward to discover these things so as to know where to work.

Some common methods for self-examination or discovering a root vice are the following:

1. Simplicity: Most 10 to 12 year olds – or even older boys who are very "young" spiritually, need an even simpler method. To do this, they jot down their top few obstacles in relationship with God, themselves and others.

2. Confession: have the boy write out his confession for a few times and bring this note in to mentoring. Go over the sins listed and see which root vice appears the most (you can also instruct him to do it himself and inform you of the result). This evidently requires two sessions, but you don't need to rush.

3. Examination Guide: Many formats exist, but here's a simple guide based on one's relationship with God, self and others. The boys need to answer the questions and give a reason *why* they act that way.

RELATIONSHIP WITH GOD: **Prayer life** and **friendship with Christ** (Do I pray? What are the difficulties I have? Which prayer commitments are the hardest? Do I know Christ and get to know him more each day?) **Sacramental life** (Mass: do I go to mass on Sundays? Weekdays? Do I live the mass as I should? Do I value Christ in the Eucharist? How is my friendship with him? Do I visit him? Confession: Do I go to confession regularly? If not, why?) **Apostolate** (Do I do apostolate? Do I give testimony of my friendship with Christ and try to bring others to know him? If not, why?)

RELATIONSHIP WITH OTHERS: **Charity** (In general do I think about other people more than myself or vice versa? Do I try to love others during the day? Do I think badly, talk badly or act unkindly?) **Family** (What difficulties do I have as a son and brother?) **Friends** (What difficulties do I have to be a good friend?) At **school**: (How do I treat classmates? teachers? My girlfriend [if applicable]?)

RELATIONSHIP WITH SELF: **Laziness** (What

personal habits do I have that could be a result of laziness?) **Vanity** (What worries me the most?) **Conscience** (Do I ever say no to my conscience?)

4. Why?: For this method, place before their eyes the goal of their lives – getting to heaven. Then go through three different categories (God, self, and others) and see what actions or attitudes they have that hold them back from reaching this goal. For example, with God some may say, "I get distracted when I pray," or "I don't like praying." Once we have a reasonable list, we need to go deeper and see the reasons behind the actions (the *why*). Ask "why?" about each obstacle to discover the root cause.

For example, "*Why do I get bored in mass? Because I am not interested in what is going on. Why am I not interested? Because I am bored and I don't like the way the church pews feel....*" In this case the root is sensuality, being uncomfortable in the pews and bored. At the end of the examination, they glance over the list and the root of each fault and they will probably find a common thread. This is usually their root vice or main issue.

5. List: This method is simply to have a list of the main manifestations or actions related to each dominant passion on a sheet you give the boy. He goes through and underlines or highlights what he feels identified with. Afterwards, you go through and see which is root vice where the majority of the manifestations are related to.

Goals: After self-examination, the second part of a rule of life after the self-examination is setting clear goals to conquer the obstacles you identified. To conquer the root sin that came up in the self-examination, we need to focus on a virtue, an ideal – how Christ lived this virtue, and a motto to motivate us.

Virtue: The best way to conquer vice is with virtue. Spending all of our time trying to avoid doing bad things is both spiritually destructive and minimalistic. The rule of life is an ounce of prevention so we don't need to provide a pound of cure later. We need to identify clearly what virtue is needed most. The simplest is the virtue that is the exact opposite of our root vice, but at times other more subtle virtues may work better: if a boy is proud, maybe charity would help him more than humility. Since love is always the strongest motivator in man, relating the virtue to love often helps. Once decided, this program is not set in stone but flexible; it is a provisional program and we will definitely change it sometime in the next year (the younger the boy, the more frequent he will need to change it). This virtue is the key to the whole program.

Ideal: the ideal is who and what they are fighting for. It is always Christ! This and the motto (next) are the motor to the reform of life. These two come from the personal experience the teen has had of Christ. In a way they are the first thing to do but I put them down here because I think they are specified by what's above. I get my ideal from my experience of Christ but each time I write a rule, I have to draw out one element of that experience as my ideal for this rule. One year my ideal may be Christ on the cross, and the next it may be Christ teaching the apostles based on what virtue I need to grow in. Yet there are so many aspects of Christ's personality to imitate, so it helps to focus on a specific event where he lived the virtue they want to conquer. For example, for those who are building generous love to fight selfishness, they could focus on Christ crucified out of love for us.

Motto: boys need to stay motivated, and that is what a slogan or motto does. It should summarize what we are seeking to achieve. It can be a phrase from the Gospel, from a saint, or a general phrase like "All for Christ." It must be very simple. For example, those working on humility may want to have something like "He must grow greater, I must grow less."[4] For those working on will power may want something like, "How can I say no in the face of such love?" Those working on self-giving might pick "If a wheat grain falls into the earth and dies, it yields a rich harvest,"[5] or those working on charity might choose, "At the evening of life, we shall be judged on our love."[6]

Concrete Steps: If the rule of life does not get into concrete details – *before I eat breakfast*, I will pray a decade of the rosary – it remains a dream and a bunch of nice thoughts. It may seem like a long path, but we are almost at the end. We are now at those concrete steps. This is the part where you think of the concrete actions or points that the boy will work on to strive to reach the virtue.

There are many ways to develop this part of the program. The most common for younger boys is to take the same outline of the relationship with God, themselves, friends, and family; then come up with a point or two in each of these categories. Older boys may want to focus a whole year of resolutions on one area. All the points should relate back to the virtue they determined as their goal. Look back at the self-examination and some concrete actions should pop out fairly easily.

You don't want something as generic as "pray more." If a boy is working on a more generous love because his root vice is selfishness, points in his rule of life could be, "morning offering before I leave my room in the morning, a Gospel reflection before dinner, and my rosary in the chapel right after school." For example, if someone is working on "will power out of love" because his root vice is laziness, points in the Program could be, "help my mom with dinner and Suzie (little sister) with homework. Complete a chore immediately when asked."

Necessary Qualities: Now that we have gone through the steps to prepare a rule of life, I outline certain qualities. If a rule of life lacks these, 'the rule of life should be adjusted.

Concrete: Each point should answer the question "when and how."

Realistic: Every point should be possible to do for the adolescent in his day to day life, not his ideal life.

Christ-centered: Each point should be directed towards their goal or virtue with the example of Christ in mind. Each point should bring him closer to Christ.

Deep and supernatural: it is a spiritual program, so we need to make sure that the long term goal is kept in mind. It cannot just be a list of actions without the reminder of why they are doing them. "Clean up the school yard out" is a nice thought, but there are deeper resolutions that help them grow in virtue, or at least give a motivation of cleaning it up out of charity to the other students.

Positive: A point should always build up and be positive, rather than negative. For example, "I will not get distracted in mass," could be rephrased as, "I will get to know Christ in each mass by paying attention and talking to Christ after communion."

Brief: The program should not be long. It should not take a lifetime to fulfill all of these points. Three to six points, no more! If a boy wants to add too many points, the mentor should help them focus on just a few of these during different periods of time. A good rule of thumb for boys is that it shouldn't be more than about half of a normal letter sized paper in standard handwriting.

Order: before going on, let's review the steps semantically:

Step 1: Establish the long term goal in life.

Step 2: Main obstacles or difficulties I have in reaching that goal with God, with others, with myself.

Step 3: What is the common thread in all these difficulties? Establish the dominant passion.

Step 4: What virtue will help me the most? Establish the virtue and goal.

Step 5: Choose an ideal and motto. What will motivate me to live this virtue?

Step 6: Write the program. What concrete resolutions (3-6) would be good for me to work on regarding that virtue in my relationship with God, with others, and with myself.

Different Formats

We need to keep in mind the purpose of a rule of life when we think of the format or method to be used. A format can definitely help some boys to visualize it, but it is ideal to go through the steps and adapt the format to the boy. I want to offer two formats and a few ideas for unique situations.

1st format: A normal basic outline is:

1. Goal
2. Virtue (objective)
3. Motto
4. Ideal (Christ...)
5. Root vice and manifestations
6. Concrete actions (there are about 50 ways to do this part)
7. Calendar (more advanced teens should review one point each night during the examination of conscience or something similar)

2nd format: For younger boys, something simpler may be appropriate:

1. Christ, the... (ideal)
2. Virtue
3. Relationship with God (one concrete action)
4. Relationship with myself (one concrete action)
5. Relationship with my family (one concrete action)
6. Relationship with my friends (one concrete action)

Simplicity keeps it short. Images or a picture of Christ can help keep them focused. It can either be handwritten or entered into some electronic device the boy sees every day. A great rule of life could be written on a napkin or an 1-screen Android note.

Special situations: Since the rule of life is centered on this teen in particular, we must adapt it for special situations.

For those dealing with a certain difficulty in life – like a divorce or death in the family – you can make a temporary rule of life for that moment. It can be simple and short. It is important to know when it is the right moment to help a person get to know themselves.

For those discerning a vocation, the program needs to include this. It could be geared towards generosity and some points can deal directly with discovering God's will in prayer and actively discerning a vocation.

Some boys may want to add a point or two extra during

Advent, or Lent to prepare them for Christmas and Easter. Instead of giving up chocolates, they add an extra act of charity each day. Summer time can also be special because the boys environment changes completely and the temptation comes to drop the formation gained during the year. Often you need to simplify or modify a rule of life based on this change of circumstances.

Put It into Practice

Our love is found in actions, not in beautiful words, so the most important part of the rule of life is putting it into practice. We should explain to teenagers how to use a rule of life once it is developed. First of all, make sure they know where it is. Keep it at hand so the boy can read it every day; don't stow it away. The rule of life helps if they do a regular examination of conscience, and is a tool for mentoring. They can also use it as a guide before confession. Some try to think of creative ways to remember each one of their points. For example, if one of the points is patience with their brothers and sisters, they could put this point on the back of their bedroom door so every time they leave their room they remember. If another is to be respectful to certain teachers at school or charitable in class, perhaps a note inside his school binder for that subject or a reminder in his locker could help.

As a mentor, the most important thing is to keep a copy. When in doubt; pull it out. This applies when preparing to mentor him, when praying and reflecting on him, or even during mentoring to review the boy's progress.

The rule of life is a key moment in mentoring: you go from doing individual actions to having a plan. You need to help the teen make this plan, but it needs to be his, not yours. (If you don't already have one yourself, I would suggest preparing one with your spiritual director.) Once a teen has such a plan, he is set to grow systematically, not just in fits and spurts.

18. GENEROSITY AND VOCATIONS

After spending a night visiting the seminary, the teens were at a nearby park playing soccer. Fr Ryan decides it is a perfect time to call the boys over one at a time to talk. First he calls Michael.

"Can we talk for a few minutes?"

Michael jogs over to the side of the field and before Fr Ryan says anything, "I want to come back this summer." Fr Ryan thinks quickly as he planned to warm up with a few general questions before asking if he was interested in joining the seminary.

"Well…" caught a little off guard, "do you know what that means? Are you ready to leave your family? Do you think God is calling you to be a priest?"

Obviously, Fr Ryan had been mentoring Michael a while, and Michael was considering the priesthood. Still this discernment was quick, the quickest I have heard of.

The vocation is ultimately an extension of generosity; he who is generous will be able to follow through if God calls, he who lacks generosity will not be able to respond.

As boys grow, they need to advance through various stages of generosity. Growth is a sign of life. If one's spiritual life is strong and well nourished, there will be growth. If a boy is progressing in his friendship with Christ and advancing on the path to holiness, he will begin to discover new things about God and new ways to serve him.

The bond of love in a relationship grows stronger over time. A relationship with God is no different, except his love is infinite. One will constantly discover new things about God's love, which will move one to want to respond with more love. This continues for all eternity.

Keep in mind that God can ask whatever he wants, whenever he wants. He knows what is best for every boy. There is little human certainty in the spiritual life. A thirteen year-old boy can have a deeper relationship with God than a fifty year-old man. Age is not a limitation for God. This is seen in young saints: St. Maria Goretti, St. Dominic Savio, St. Agnes, St. Tarcisius, and Blessed José Luis Sánchez del Río, to name but a few. God can ask sanctity of a youth and grant him the grace to achieve it. There may be some cases where the boys you direct have an even deeper prayer life than you. They could be dealing with more difficult situations than you have ever dealt with in your life, and they could show an incredible amount of virtue. This does not change the fact that God has also asked you to guide this person spiritually, as an instrument of his grace and love. No matter what, you have the *grace of state* as their mentor, so you are the proper instrument for the Holy Spirit.

'I give an outline of the steps of generosity, then discuss vocational discernment so that you can help those who are called.

Degrees of Generosity

As you mentor a boy, he will grow in generosity one way or another. He may dedicate a few more minutes to prayer, he may help mom out at home, or he may take on a more demanding service project. To help see this path, we can divide it into different steps. Two Gospel stories show us the steps diversely: one interiorly or personally, and one exteriorly or institutionally.

In John 4, Jesus carries on a discussion with a Samaritan woman at the well[1] which shows the different degrees of interior generosity that a boy should go through. These levels are personal – they are the degree of trust that the boy gives to you as a mentor and to Jesus. Usually going through all five takes months, not minutes, but Jesus can work a lot faster than us – he's God, we aren't.

1) **Goodwill or Affinity,** *the two are on speaking terms.* "Jesus said to her, 'Give me a drink.'" Jesus is breaking customs to talk with her and her response shows she is willing to talk. This is what you need to start mentoring: the boy is willing to speak with you and with Jesus.

2) **Friendship,** *a relationship where both want to continue because they care about each other.* "If you knew the gift of God, and who it is that is saying to you 'give me a drink,' you would have asked him and he would have given you living water." Jesus is opening up salvation to her, and she asks, "give me this water." Immediately from the first time you mentor a boy, he needs to feel that you care, that Jesus cares. He rarely will want to continue the relationship if you don't express interest.

3) **Trust,** *the boy trusts you and Jesus with his secrets.* Jesus pushes her with the request, "Go call your husband," but she shows her trust by admitting she has none. After a boy has grown a little and trusts you with his secrets, you can motivate him and ask him something: invite him to a weekend retreat, suggest a service project to him, or ask him some special' act of virtue.

4) **Invitation and Decision,** *now the boy is ready to make a decision for Christ.* She shows her openness with a question about the Messiah and Jesus says, "I who speak to you am he." A boy can now be asked to make some kind of formal commitment or to take on some small responsibility – this is the beginning of the depth-confidence we spoke of earlier.

5) **Surrender,** *total self-giving to Christ.* She "left her water jar, and went away into the city and said to the people, 'Come, see a man who told me all that I ever did. Can this be the Christ?'" This is the attitude of one surrendered to Christ. At this point a boy can be asked some serious commitment like becoming a youth leader or taking on a major responsibility, such as organizing a whole apostolate.

Jesus told another story that we all remember: "A sower went out to sow. And as he sowed, some seeds fell along the path... Other seeds fell on rocky ground... Other seeds fell upon thorns... Other seeds fell on good soil." In the parable of the sower[2] we see the different levels of external generosity which we can link with various levels of commitment in the Church. These levels follow upon the internal levels. These levels are helpful when you are getting to know a boy to determine where he and his family fit in so you can better mentor him. As you accompany him through the stages of internal generosity, these external stages should be a guide to show he is truly growing.

1) *Find and prepare rich soil:* **A person of good will**. These people are all around. Here we are not looking for something fantastic, but someone who shows up for Sunday mass or even a non-Catholic who wants to do something good.

2) *Sow the seed of the Gospel:* **A Catholic who participates**. This includes those moderately involved in a parish such as attending Sunday Mass, showing up for youth group. When you start out with most boys they will be here since you will usually be working through the youth group. Joining the youth group is usually a first step in external generosity.

3) *Cultivate its growth:* **An active Catholic**. This is those going beyond basic involvement. A boy begins to grow beyond just showing up to making a serious commitment to prayer and apostolate. Here a boy starts to want mentoring and not just accept it. Now they make the next commitment in generosity: they become an official member of the youth

club, they pray, they promote Christ.

4) *Bring in the harvest:* **Apostles at the service of the Church**. This is someone who is dedicated to spreading Christ's kingdom. In most cases we aren't talking about an employed missionary but someone who spreads Christ through the ordinary everyday events of life – this is where we want to lead the boys. At this stage, a boy might be willing to give a summer as a volunteer, and the question of a religious or priestly vocation will often arise.

Vocational Discernment

The waitress shows Sam and his old mentor to a seat in Bob Evans. As they sit down and order, Fr Donald begins,

"So how was your year at the boarding school?"

"I really liked it, and I liked the priests and brothers who run it…"

"I thought you'd like them when we agreed you were going there. You wanted to see if God was calling you."

"I think he is, but not to be part of your community. I mean I love you all and I like all the retreats, but I just don't think it's for me. I want to stay close to home, all this formality just doesn't fit super-well with me. I already spoke to Fr Steve [the diocesan vocation director] and he recommended I take one year of college at our St. Mary's College and see him every month. I'll join the seminary next year."

"I think that's great. You tried and my community didn't fit for you. You know I'm in the area if you want to have coffee. I figure Fr Steve will probably be a better spiritual director now than I would be since he's diocesan. At the seminary you will find some other diocesan priests who are directors."

"Thanks. I thought you would be worried."

"Why? I want you to get to heaven, if God is calling you to be a diocesan priest, that's the way."

Just then the waitress comes with bacon and eggs for Sam and biscuits and gravy for Fr Donald. They keep chatting for 2 hours reminiscing on all the adventures they had: the time Sam got smothered by his buddies on the couch, the time they set up a slip and slide and then threw the dog on, and the time Sam spent all lunch wondering where his watch was only to find he sat on it. That was the last time Fr Donald mentored Sam, but it was the fruit of the fifty times he had mentored him before.

Every Catholic has the responsibility to promote vocations and help the Church. The Knights of Columbus always say: "Vocations Are Everybody's Business." Vocations are the lifeblood of the Church; they offer the sacraments and testify to the other side, to heaven. The vocation is the greatest gift God can give a human being; it is the source of the deepest joy and peace this side of heaven for the individual as well. Just think of those tears of joy every new priest – and most parents of new priests – shed during their first mass.

For those priests ordained in 2011, "On average… they were about 16 when they first considered a vocation to the priesthood." [3] As a mentor you are dealing with souls right at this age, so you have a greater responsibility here. Vocational discernment is an extension of what we have already covered not a totally different subject. When we help teens grow closer to Christ and more generous, this will lead some to consider a priestly or consecrated vocation. I'm not talking about putting up signs or asking teens to stand up at the end of a youth event. Instead, we have to consider one-on-one dialogue with a teen that is already relatively advanced in generosity.

This section will present the three elements of a vocation and concrete steps you can take as a mentor. The best guides I have found are *Peter on the Shore* and *Vocation: questions & answers*, both by Fr Anthony Bannon, LC, which are free on vocation.com. If you want more, you can check them out.

For any vocation there must be three elements: the qualities, the call, and the response. If a boy has only one or two of these elements, you need to admit that something is missing. If a boy has the qualities and wants to be generous with God, we should encourage him to give God the first chance – he may hear the call soon. The majority of those who consider a vocation don't enter a seminary and only about half who enter are actually ordained. Giving God the first chance does not mean he has a vocation; it means giving God first dibs on his heart.

The qualities: For a boy to have a vocation to the priesthood or consecrated life, he needs to be a normal boy:

- On a human level, they need to have good health, a firm will or the potential to develop a strong will, as well as a normal and healthy physical demeanor.

- They need average or above average intelligence. Becoming a priest requires about 8 years of University-level study in North America. Non-priestly religious orders vary on this, and some communities are stricter based on their mission.

- They should have a strong and healthy psychology, "Ability to weather the normal stress involved in the vocation; freedom from illness, addictions, psychosis, neurosis, or obsessions."[4]

- Spiritually, they should also have a great desire to love Christ and want to be holy. They should be capable adapting to different circumstances, living charity and live team life in a community. They need some spiritual maturity, "This means that you are not too recent a convert, not given to strange devotions, that you give God his place, have an active faith in the Church as Christ founded it."[5]

- There are certain difficulties that do not negate a vocation but mean that it would generally be better to wait till the teen matures or the problems disappear depending on the type. If you suspect a boy may fit in this category, ask a local priest who knows about these and supports high school seminaries.

The call: The call is something that only the individual called can prove, and he can't always. It is an illumination on the soul by the Holy Spirit; either immediate or over a period of time. It is not tangible or easily explained, it is mysterious for the teen and often more so for you. If you're married, think of how over a certain period of time, or at a certain moment it clicked and you realize this girl is the one you want to spend the rest of your life with. The call to follow God completely is the most beautiful gift a boy can ever receive. The call has 3 elements:

The first element is a kind of revelation, a certainty of the path God wants for him. It is either sudden or a certainty from prayer over a time. Often the idea of being a priest starts to bother him and he denies he ever felt the call. In this case, try to help him discover the call again. The vocational discernment process is something between God and the soul, although he usually uses normal human circumstances; divine visions are rare. Help him to be sincere and see his whole life in God's wondrous plan. God never contradicts himself, so usually the best advice is to have him pray more in those moments of doubt and ask God for the grace to see clearly if he has a call.

A second element is a certain restlessness or uneasiness regarding the vocation. The person is sensitive when it comes to the topic of a vocation. Some boys can be around priests, religious, or consecrated persons for years and the thought of the vocation never crosses their mind. Every once in a while, a boy will have a different kind of reaction and feel drawn to that vocation. This shows there is a degree of spiritual sensibility towards Christ, and a consecrated vocation. There is a "spiritual motive. This means that in looking into the vocation you are motivated by something more than human convenience or ambition – a desire to save souls, to use your life in the most pleasing way to God, to bring God's mercy to others, more concern for what you are called to be than what you are called to do."[6]

Thirdly, you can look for the specific signs of a vocational call. They are those special sentiments, sensations and occasions that call us to do something more. God puts desires in our heart so that he can fulfill them; certain desires lead a boy down the path to a vocation. Here a few questions to ask a boy: What are you doing for God and others? Are you satisfied with what you are doing, with what you are? Do you need something else to be happy? Do you have clear goals in life? In the face of a certain situation, what do you think God is trying to tell you? What do you think God wanted out of that situation?

A boy can feel overwhelmed and lack generosity because he sees himself unworthy. We are all unworthy and incapable, but God gives the grace to those he calls. Jesus tells us: "You have not chosen me but I have chosen you."[7]

God is not tricky, he is clear. If he wants someone to follow the call; he will show them it is the way if they walk the path of virtue and ask him with faith. You need to help the boys open themselves to discover what God is trying to tell them.

The response: It is a "yes" or a "no." "Maybe" is not a valid answer with regard to a vocation; just imagine if your wife said that when you asked her to marry you. ("Not yet" can sometimes be valid, as my dad found out the first two times he asked mom to marry him.) A boy should be generous and have the attitude of accepting God's will in everything; he is God and we are not. When a boy discovers the call of God, a battle of generosity begins inside. We need to help him be generous enough to give God everything, keeping before his eyes the beauty of God's call. When a boy looks back at the end of life, this path will be worth more than any worldly profession. God knows what is best and what will make us happy in life. The grace of saying "yes" to God requires much prayer. There can be a long and arduous battle in the soul trying to respond to God's call. As the boy gets closer to God, he will realize Jesus' words: "my yoke is easy, and my burden is light."[8]

When a teen should respond to God's call depends on many factors. God can call someone when he is a small boy and he may need that boy to wait many years before leaving home. On average, newly ordained religious priests knew members of their community 6 years before entering the seminary.[9] No matter what the length of the response, you need to help the boy persevere in his love for Christ and with his generous response.

What you can do: The most important thing a mentor can

do is show teens the vocation as a possibility. Mentors can help teens grow in generosity, they can help teens when the vocation arises, they can help the family, and they can hand the teen on to someone who lives that specific vocation.

"It is much more important to *prepare* yourself for your vocation than to *discern* it. God can give you in a flash the awareness you need in order to see it. But what happens then?"[10] This was in a way how I discovered my vocation. I was the sacristan at the University and regular at daily mass and various activities, but I was so set on marriage that one of the factors in choosing my major was how well it would support a big family. Then, one Sunday after mass we had a presentation on World Youth Day; when I heard John Paul II say "Be not afraid to be the saints of the new millennium," something changed inside me and I knew God was calling me to the priesthood.

In other words, generosity is the key, beyond discerning the specific call from God. If God calls, one's response is determined by one's level of generosity. If one isn't generous, it doesn't matter if God calls, because the person isn't going anywhere. Generosity will never be wasted because even if he is called to a different vocation, such as marriage, his growth in generosity will help him. This generosity needs to be made concrete. With anyone who is considering a vocation, even at a young age, you need to help him with a demanding but realistic rule of life.

As a boy grows in generosity, very often the idea of a vocation will arise. Usually, the idea arises in those most generous and dedicated among the boys in the youth group. Sometimes it arises in a middle-of-the-road teen, but in such a case, the teen's increased generosity should be asked for before you need to take the call seriously. In general, vocation discernment should not be seen as a separate activity from everything else you do in mentoring, but the natural progression for some boys once they reach a certain level of generosity.

Just because a guy considers a vocation does not mean he's

called; just as not because a guy goes out with a girl is he called to marry her. Sometimes, the vocation will arise at a young age, fade into the background, and then come to life again. The call of many younger teens lacks depth, so don't be naïvely enthusiastic and push them towards a vocation. But on the other hand, we never know if it is a true vocation. Be extra attentive with such boys because they generally are more spiritually sensitive. God calls today! The case we think most obvious may not be the same for God.

Watch the family and parents of such a boy; if they strongly discourage the vocation it is unlikely he will follow it. Unless you have a son or daughter who followed a vocation, you can't answer most of the family's questions. First of all, encourage the boy to talk to his parents regarding this interest. It is much easier for them to understand what he is going through and support him if they have been aware from day one. At times, parents can be surprised but are often suspicious. Little by little, the boy needs to help his parents understand what he feels, why he feels it, and what he wants to do to respond to the call of God. As a mentor, you need to make sure that the parents know that you are there as a support for their son to grow in his spiritual life. They need to know that only God can give someone a vocation, we can only help a person discern and follow God's path. If the parents oppose the possible vocation of their son, and the boy feels very strongly that it is God's will, you need to be very delicate. It is a process that both the family and the boy need to go through, all in God's time.

Precise discernment usually works best when entrusted to someone who lives the specific vocation that interests the teen. Generally, someone following the life the boy is interested in will do it best; a Carmelite if he wants to be a Carmelite, a Legionary if the Legionaries of Christ interest him, or likewise a diocesan priest.

As a good mentor, you should be aware of the vocational options, at least in general. What religious communities could you suggest? Is there a high school seminary nearby you could present if a boy is seriously considering the vocation at a young age? What is the number and e-mail for the diocesan vocation director?

Mentors need to help teens progress in internal generosity like the woman at the well. When teens progress internally, they should also do so externally. For some teens, this progress will cause the vocational question to arise and for the chosen few, a mentor can help them discover God's call.

19. SOME CLOSING THOUGHTS

As we began with the story of the crucifixion, we come full circle. Even when everything seems to go wrong, every storm cloud has a silver lining. On Calvary, Christ was abandoned by all but a few. Even after he rose his few followers huddled in a tiny room, scared that the authorities were going to break down the door and arrest them at any moment.

But that moment was the moment of victory. Christ now has more followers that anyone else (2.1 billion Christians to be precise). Often God uses our failures in mentoring to bring out a good result we couldn't have imagined: I know one case where a mentor thought a particular session scared a teen off from youth group, but then saw the same teen enter the seminary two years later. We can never lose hope like the apostles did, but we must trust in God's grace working through us on his schedule.

Life is a rollercoaster ride during the teenage years. Augustine, one of the Church's greatest minds, had a mistress for thirteen years.[1] Eventually the incessant prayers of St Monica moved his heart to convert. We may lose the battle today, but the book of revelation already gives us the end of the war: Christ conquers evil. No matter what happens with a teen, God's grace can still work. Keep trying to help them.

We can also easily lose hope about our own abilities. After this book we think we know everything, then reality hits a month later when a boy asks us something we don't really know the answer to. We only learn by practice and by minor falls like this. Just tell the boy you'll answer him next time and search for an answer in the meantime. St Alphonsius Ligouri says, "The directing of souls is the art of arts,"[2] so it is not going to come to us in a week, a month, or even a year. However, if we try our best and pray, somehow the Holy Spirit makes up for our deficiencies.

Now you are trained to help a boy out via mentoring. All we learned can be summarized in a phrase: listen to the Holy Spirit, and when he isn't clear, follow the guidelines from this book. Usually the Holy Spirit follows the general guidelines laid out here, but it would be impossible for me – and dead boring for you – to lay out every possible scenario. I trust your own reason and the light of the Holy Spirit.

Remember that mentoring is a great means for *you* to get to heaven along with the boys. All the spiritual authors agree that working for the salvation of other souls is one of the best ways to assure our own salvation.

Despite all these difficulties, never lose the focus: we are doing this to help boys become saints. Quality and holiness are more important than number, because a few saints will change the world. Just look at the twelve. As Fr Frederick Faber mentions, "One saint is worth a million common Catholics."[3]

In the end, mentoring is simple. Love the teens you mentor, show them Christ's love, and teach them to love Christ. The rest is details.

APPENDICES

I want to provide you with material that you can apply
practically in your own mentoring of teenagers.

A. THE FOUR QUALITIES OF A MENTOR

We want to form boys into (1) virtuous, (2) prayerful (3) Catholic (4) leaders. Mentoring is a key part of this achievement. Since many pages have already been written, I give a brief outline of the four here. It goes without saying that this is not minimalism, as just doing the minimum goes against the whole spirit of mentoring. Don't read this as a checklist but as general guidelines. '

Virtue: You need to be able to direct and not be directed. The first step of this is being a model of virtue for the boys.

- Live all the Christian virtues to the degree you avoid all moral sin and most venial sin.

- Maturity and willpower that allow you to be loyal, keep the right emotional distance, and remain in control. You need to have a heart to help the boys and be willing to adapt to their personalities.

- You need to be a clear communicator, and know how to be discreet.

- You need to have a regular marital state (single, consecrated, or married in the Church).

Prayer: You need to pray more than you ask the boys to. If you are a relatively faithful member of a lay movement or third order, your commitments should provide at least this minimum level. If not, here is a basic summary of minimal prayer that should be expected:

- At least 20 minutes daily dedicated to prayer
  - Minimum 8-10 minutes of this in non-structured dialogue with Christ, the other persons of the Trinity, or the Blessed Mother (meditation, conscience exam, Gospel reflection, a visit to the Eucharist, etc.)
  - Include daily mass if you attend
  - This may seem like a lot but add up all the little prayers you say and you will be surprised
- Sunday Mass and communion
- Regular Confession (minimum every 2 months)
- A personal relationship with Jesus Christ based on faith, hope and love; not just what has been handed on but something you live yourself.
- A focus on major devotions (Rosary, Mass, Gospel, Liturgy of the Hours, Divine Mercy, etc.) and excessively focused on odd devotions that can distort the spiritual life (for example basing the main thrust of your spiritual life on some unapproved apparition or visionary even after some bishops have said not to, or placing an attachment on some particular prayer above the mass, the Gospel, or obedience in the Church).
  - A basic knowledge of these main devotions (even those that aren't your thing)
- A weekend-long retreat every year or two
- A spiritual director that you see at least twice a year

Catholic: This is probably the simplest to explain: if you are mentoring Catholic teens, we must assume that you are Catholic. This means you believe all that is taught by the Church in the Catechism (including *Humane Vitae*), not that you follow all the theological trends.

Leader: leading means influencing others. For mentoring, this means that the boys look up to you or want to be like you, and that you are able to relate with them. Among adults, you should also be a contributing team member. Jim Collins describes 5 levels of leadership[1] and anything from level 2 and up is sufficient to be a mentor. In other words you need to know teamwork.

1. Highly Capable Individual
2. Contributing Team Member
3. Competent Manager
4. Effective Leader
5. Executive

To be a mentor, you need virtue, prayer, Catholic identity, and leadership. But there is one more thing: competence. This course will teach competence, but the other four qualities you need to either have or develop on your own. If you are not sure if you have what it takes, the best advice I could give is to check with your own spiritual director or a priest who you know and trust.

B. Year by Year Psychology and Formation

Here is an attempt to make the areas of development and formation concrete year by year. Unfortunately it is long. (It is best to read chapters 6 through 10, or at least 8 and 9 before reading this so you are not overwhelmed.) To try and make it somewhat manageable, I have put it in a list format. Generally, one area of development is followed by one area of formation that most relates to it, although 'they don't correspond perfectly. At times the ages overlap because growth is much more an organic process rather than a step-by-step. Often ages below 10 are included; they should provide a basis for what we see in mentoring.

1) **Physiological:** Body change uses a lot of energy and leaves teens exhausted. Early or late maturation is socially awkward. Be aware that some boys may tend to get worked up abou these changes and you may need to help them calm down and see all the changes not just this.

   a) **Birth to 11:** Boys and girls seem almost identical
   b) **11 to 13:** Pre-pubescence: first distinction between sexes.
   c) **13 to 16:** Pubescence: sexual material produced (by 14

sexual temptations become more acute).

    d) **16 to 20:** Post-pubescence: final changes like facial hair, the change process slows down.

2) **Friendship:** This is the primary environment where boys live, but because changes happen rapidly, boys usually do best socializing with those of their own age.

    a) **Birth to 10:** Anybody I meet who doesn't hit me is my friend

    b) **10-15:** Interpersonal relationships explored but begin at a superficial level. At 11 or 12 they live for their friends, so we must win over the leader and provide real friendship in the youth ministry we are offering.

    c) **15-20:** True friendship which becomes intimate. Seek female friends around 15 but exclusive girlfriends must be delayed till personality is complete.

3) **Intellectual Ability:** Children develop progressively from the age of reason, slowly being able to grasp things on a more abstract, less concrete plane through reflection.

    a) **About 7:** he reaches the age of reason and can distinguish reality from imagination.

    b) **10 to 13:** Still thinks primarily in images with a very lively imagination. Moves strongly in the direction of formal logic due to first self-reflection. Strong memory but still impulsive.

    c) **13 to 14:** Self-centered so tends to flee reality and be the great system-maker but always "misunderstood."

    d) **14 to 15:** Now sufficient reflection to define oneself, able to reflect objectively on truths received. Spends a lot of time in his interior world.

    e) **15 to 16:** Becomes independent because personality is fairly defined. Able to compartmentalize Christ. Can relate abstract concepts.

    f) **16 to 20:** Still develops and rounds out his personality making the existing connections firm.

4) **Intellectual Formation:** Teenage boys need a logical thinking process, certain basic knowledge of faith, morals, prayer, and the ability to communicate one's convictions.

a) **7 to 11:** Needs to know that the Bible and saint stories are true (not fairy tales).

b) **11 to 14:** Knowledge and retention are central; they are memorizers driven by competition. Present the basics of the Catechism the Bible.

c) **13 to 15:** Boys need to see truth as useful for them but then move beyond this to be motivated objectively.

d) **14 to 15:** Deepen their knowledge so as to communicate it.

e) **15 to 17:** Interiorize material so as to become convinced. He needs to analyze current issues with truths of the faith.

f) **16 to 19:** Needs firm intellect by college or it will be a waste of time.

5) **Emotional / Psychological Development:** Adolescence is a turbulent time for the boy's emotions; but we must lead the boy must towards emotional stability and a firm will.

a) **1 to 11:** Childish psychology based on immediate experience.

b) **11 to 13:** Tend to be vain and self-focused but can become enthusiastic for Christ.

c) **13 to 14:** A lot of self-promoting tendencies need to be directed in the right place. He needs to understand passions to overcome them.

d) **14 to 15:** Spiritual cooling here can become definitive so he needs to live his relationship with God as a response to his love. His manner of living the faith must be valued and lived with stability.

e) **15 to 17:** Maturation stabilizes. He can now become more focused on his mission in Christ's Church. Pragmatism becomes a large threat.

f) **16 to 19:** Emotions stabilize and energy returns.

6) **Human Formation:** A teenage boy must know himself and develop certain faculties (will, firm emotions, manners, and conscience) so as to be a leader who brings people to Christ.

a) **1 to 8:** Obedience to what parents ask.
b) **7 to 11:** Needs to learn and follow a solid set of rules.
c) **11 to 13:** A boy must be sincere (truth defines the authentic man) and obedient: forming his will and giving himself to others like Christ.
d) **13 to 14:** Now morality is not just rules or obedience but in the conscience. Mentoring should provide him with concrete conscience formation. Now he must decide on a sure model for life and realize he is responsible for his own life.
e) **14 to 15:** He needs to become objective – you should help form his conscious in this regard. If he wants to be a spiritual leader, which he should, he must commit himself to continual growth.
f) **15 to 17:** He needs to live by his convictions, to become an effective leader. He now has enough reflection to realize his temperament and apply it to his whole life. He should now be able to share virtues and not just live them.
g) **16 to 20:** If you have been following them, they can now be launched into the mission. Otherwise, you may need to go through some of the previous formation.

7) **Moral Development:** From birth to adulthood, a boy grows in his understanding of morality on various levels. Boys will be moved by an equal or higher level but not a lower one.

a) **1 to 7:** Punishment is bad, otherwise it's good.
b) **7 to 11:** Good promises a reward, bad doesn't.
c) **10 to 15 (Conventional):** first they try to conform to a group (well-defined roles are essential) and later they realize the common good and become legalistic (you need to avoid extremes here). Any youth program needs to be presented as the group to conform to.
d) **15 to 20 (Post-conventional):** they pursue the moral law beyond loyalty to a group and need to see the common good to avoid legalistic interpretations.

8) **Spiritual Formation:** During the teen years they begin to ask the big questions. They need to be shown Christ as the friend above and beyond all human friendships. We need to help them see beyond – it should not be abnormal that a boy considers a life dedicated to religion.

   a) **1 to 10:** needs heroes and saints as models (thinks only in images).

   b) **11 to 14:** Open but seek immediate gratification or answer to prayers. Needs to see God's will, not just human authority. This stage is usually a boy's last attachment to mom so it's a time to develop filial attachment to Mary. Needs personal relationship with Jesus through prayer and the sacraments.

   c) **13 to 15:** Boys *solidify their image of God* at this age. They will participate in religious acts for pleasure over profundity but need to see spiritual things as satisfying their needs.

   d) **14 to 16:** Friendship with Christ is the pearl of great price. True friendship with God is found by uniting his will to live authentically for him. He must now resolve any lingering doubts about his faith to unite with the Church.

   e) **15 to 17:** A rule of life (see chapter 17) becomes indispensable to see how he can truly change the world by channeling their passions into radical love for Christ and to base his spiritual life on interior conviction not circumstances.

   f) **16 to 20:** A deep personal relationship with Christ should be developed.

9) **Motivation and View of Christ:** We must always be positive in our motivations; there is only one model worth building your life on, Jesus Christ.

   a) **1 to 4:** Parental affection.

   b) **5 to 7:** Hero for God.

   c) **8 to 11:** Friend of God.

   d) **11 to 13:** Christ is presented as the leader with great enthusiasm.

e) **13 to 15:** Motivation must be made personal according to his interests and intensified. Christ can be presented as a guide or friend. The boy now needs an intense personal experience of Christ to grow.

f) **15 to 17:** Christ the Apostle invites the boy to be an apostle: apostolate can now be ambitious.

g) **16 to 20:** The needs of the world and souls, the love of Christ, etc., can be the motivations which should now be firmly rooted as convictions.

10) **Apostolate:** One of the most important things to help boys mature is "depth-confidence" (see chapter 10): we trust kids to do apostolate (or other things) even though a certain percentage of their first experiences will meet with failure. Boys are self-centered, seeing themselves as an essential link in mankind's salvation. Any youth ministry needs to take advantage of this notion.

a) **1 to 9:** The boy can accompany older boys and parents on service projects.

b) **10 or 11:** The boys can begin doing their own apostolates but with guidance from adults or older teens.

c) **11 to 13:** He has loads of energy for service projects but is used to wasting time. Apostolate should be as a team. Needs to see the value of the soul so as to have personal commitment.

d) **13 to 14:** He needs to see the leadership Christ is asking him personally. Present him apostolates and give him a positive experience in order to make a serious and regular commitment to apostolate.

e) **14 to 16:** Ideally, he should commit himself to demanding apostolic activity which will interiorize his convictions. Some boys will be ready for ambitious apostolate requiring leadership.

f) **15 to 17:** He should feel actively responsible for the Church's future so he will attract others. He needs to dedicate himself all the more to apostolate so as to leave a mark before going to heaven.

g) **16 to 20:** Change this world for Christ!

11) **Mentors:** Needs to be a leader to the teens. A confidant and a reference point for the boys.

   a) **1 to 5:** Parents should take full responsibility.

   b) **5 to 10:** Formation should be in the group not generally individual.

   c) **11 to 13:** He needs to see you as the reference point in his life. Make him an active participant of formation – he is not given it but "gets" it (acquires it as an active agent).

   d) **13 to 15:** You take on the role of the guide; firm with good reasons and put up with his "rebellion."

   e) **14 to 16:** Listen when he opens up. Tends to be emotional and frustrated and often mistaken left as a "lost cause." Must be an authentic confidant whom he can go to as he wants someone other than his parents.

   f) **15 to 17:** Detach emotionally so the boy works on his own steam. You must be meticulously prepared with answers and natural moral ascendancy. His faith and youth ministry needs to be who he is, not just one of many things he does.

Between 16 and 20: Switch from mentoring (forming him so he can discover God's will) to spiritual direction (the discovery and discernment of God's will).

C. 99 Simple Resolutions

As we help boys grow, we need to give them small concrete resolutions based on their behavior.[1] Sometimes at the beginning you will deal with serious behavior he needs to correct. However, this should pass away, and then we need short term goals. To work short term goals:

1) Need to match with his rule of life.
2) Need to be attainable by the next time you see him (2 weeks or a month).
3) Need to be measurable.
4) Need to challenge the boy.
5) Need to be useful.
6) Need to be daily practices not once a week.
7) Need to be given with spiritual motivation.

Here is a list of 99 short term goals that you can use with teens; they are inter-related as often one resolution will help out several areas. They are not the only ones but should be a general guide. Some are more appropriate for certain ages, for instance once a boy is in High School we should help him work properly without parental oversight while a younger teen can often be helped by more.

Progressive steps to begin a personal prayer life:

1) Pray short morning prayers (for example: Our Father, Hail Mary, and Glory Be).
2) Pray short morning and night prayers.
3) Spend 3 minutes a day reading the lives of the saints or the Gospels.
4) Pray a decade of the rosary every day (or a Divine Mercy Chaplet).
5) Expand your reading time to 5 minutes and include reflection upon the text of the Gospels.
6) Make a two minute examination of conscience with night prayers to your successes and failures, and make one resolution to improve tomorrow.
7) Make a short visit to the Eucharist or spiritual communion.
8) Increase your vocal prayers a little (a second decade of the rosary, one psalm with night prayers…)
9) Increase your nightly conscience exam to 5 minutes.
10) Increase your time dedicated to Gospel reflection (this can be in stages as high school teens should be able to do 20 minutes but increase it 5 minutes at a time).

To cultivate the presence of God:
11) Make a special visit to the Eucharist each day.
12) Silence from when you finish your night prayers till breakfast (no iPod, no radio, no harassing little sisters…).
13) Make 3 short prayers to remind you of God's presence throughout the day.
14) Make a short prayer before beginning any activity.
15) Remind yourself of your Gospel reflection whenever you are alone (waiting for the bus, doing chores…).
16) Make a personal schedule and stick to it (this may seem out of place, but having a schedule takes our mind off other concerns so we can focus on what really matters).

To cultivate a prayer life:
17) Say your prayers with attention; really mean what you say.
18) Keep a prayer notebook and write down your resolution from your conscience exam and a note on your Gospel reflection each day.

19) Get a picture of Jesus or Mary and say your prayers before it.
20) Place something plainly in view to remind you to say your prayers every day.
21) Say one prayer a day with someone else (morning prayers with mom, a decade of the rosary with your buddies on the bus…).
22) Thank Jesus for 3 things each day.

To cultivate generosity:

23) Share candy at recess or lunch.
24) Let the other guy go first through the door.
25) Offer your seat to others, when allowed.
26) Lend something you know a friend admires (pen, skateboard, iPod…).
27) When you lend something, don't ask for it back; only take it when your friend offers it.
28) Give two candies whenever a classmate or friend asks for one.
29) Offer to help someone carry something once a day.
30) Pick up anything that others drop (pens, books, etc.).
31) Help your sibling with a chore that isn't yours.
32) Do a hidden act of service for mom.
33) Dedicate 10 minutes every afternoon to making your siblings happy.

To cultivate responsibility:

34) Arrive 30 seconds early to something you are usually late for (first class after lunch…).
35) Pick up two pieces of trash before leaving each classroom.
36) Ask your parents for an extra chore.
37) Keep your notes tidy; organize them once you get home, before you play.
38) Set the table for dinner once you get home before playing.
39) Silence in class.
40) Do what you are supposed to be doing better when nobody is watching (homework, cleanliness…).
41) Make a special effort to make a good sign of the cross when you pray before every meal.

42) Perfect order in your things: locker, backpack, room.

43) Collect the wrappers when your friends finish their candy.

To cultivate obedience:

44) When mom or dad asks you to do something, stop immediately and do it.

45) If you see you are about to be asked something (silence in class, cleaning your room…), do it before you are asked.

46) As soon as you finish something, report back and ask if there is anything else.

47) Offer to do something that needs doing once a day (clean the whiteboards in class, sweep off the porch…).

48) Make a special effort to do whatever you are asked well.

To cultivate willpower: Here special care is needed to make sure they are not harmful. Kids need lots of energy and to be clean. It is always better that a boy eats more spinach than skip desert.

49) Set an alarm on your watch for the end of prayer time when you begin and don't look at it while you pray.

50) Willingly do something you don't like (trade lunches with a boy for a lunch that isn't as tasty).

51) Pack fruit over candy in your lunchbox.

52) Get out of bed at the first instant.

53) Keep your shirt always tucked in (even during sports).

54) Keep your hair tidy (this one doesn't work if the kid is vain).

55) Always wait till at least 2 others begin eating before you start.

56) Offer a piece of your candy to others before taking a piece yourself.

57) Make a visit to the Eucharist every day just to say "hello" (this assumes the boy has a chapel at school or close to home).

58) Keep your hands out of your pockets.

59) Don't lean on walls.

60) Keep your feet proper while seated.

61) Sing as well as you can during mass (school mass or Sunday mass).

62) Sweat during sports.
63) Ask the teacher to check your notebook each day after your least-preferred class (make sure that this will be appreciated at his school before asking it).
64) Walk properly, don't shuffle.

To cultivate external discipline:

65) Stand straight, don't slouch.
66) Sit up straight when seated.
67) Raise your hand and wait to be called in class and your club.
68) Use "please," "thank you," and "excuse me" even with friends.
69) Politely greet all adults throughout the day. Use "Sir" and "Ma'am" if you don't know their names.

To cultivate constancy:

70) Say your prayers every single day, not just most days.
71) Pick a chore that requires extra effort and give full effort the whole time to finish it.
72) Apply a short term goal for a few months.
73) Aim for 15% higher grade on the next assignment in the subject you like least.

To cultivate sincerity:

74) Make a real effort to overcome laziness once a day.
75) Recall your short term goal at lunch and before bed.
76) Recall your short-term goal or rule of life before getting out of bed.
77) When your parents or teachers are not there, ask what you would do were they there, and then adjust your behavior accordingly.
78) Before bed, note one area you slipped up on and make a firm decision to improve tomorrow.
79) Apologize before the day ends when you offend someone.

To cultivate initiative:

80) Help someone every day.
81) Figure out a way to speed up something and apply it (morning shower, taking out the trash…).
82) Get interested in something new (try out a new sport at

recess, go to a few meetings of the chess club…).

83) Learn about a schoolmate's family.

84) Invent a new competition and propose it to your friends.

To cultivate a spirit of hard work:

85) If you are distracted in prayer, make up the time.

86) Do all your homework well, and without stalling.

87) Do your household chores quickly and ask mom for an extra.

88) Ask a parent to review your homework in a subject you dislike.

89) Make sure you have all you need before starting (textbook, pen, notebook…).

90) Take immediate action when distracted. If distracted during homework stand up, if you are stalling in the shower, turn up the cold water.

91) Keep your things dust and junk free (desk, bedroom floor…)

92) Dedicate yourself to improving one skill in sports.

93) Leave every place better than you found it (pick up trash, turn off the lights, organize the desks…).

To cultivate manners:

94) Do not reach across the table.

95) Always serve one other (a little sister for example) before serving yourself.

96) Compliment one person once a day.

97) Compliment two people twice a day.

98) Avoid doing something that might be annoying (if the teen doesn't think of something immediately, help him out).

99) Open the door for friends, classmates and family members.

D. A Model Guide Sheet

Here is the *friendship* guide sheet as an example of a guide sheet you could use with the boys you mentor.[1] (This is just the questions without the space for answers in the original.)

1. **Name one of your closest friends, and then list 3 reasons why this person is a good friend.**

2. **Read the following, and respond with Y (Yes), N (No), or M (Maybe):**

    a. I would like to have more friends. _____

    b. I think I can be a good friend to others. _____

    c. I choose the right kind of friends. _____

    d. My closest friends should be practicing Catholic. _____

    e. Sometimes my friends are a bad influence on me. _____

    f. I have a hard time making friends. _____

    g. I wish I had a best friend. _____

    h. My friends make me sin or do things I regret later. _____

    i. I want to trade in the friends I have for some new ones. _____

    j. My parents don't like my friends. _____

k.   My friends talk about me behind my back. _____
l. I have a few friends at this camp. _____

3. **Circle the more true answer.** *When I'm with my friends...*

a....I usually get them to do what I want to do.
b.   ...They usually get me to do what they want to do.

4. **Read these Bible passages and complete the sentences:**

a.*Now when three of Job's friends heard of all the misfortune that had come upon him, they set out each one from his own place: Eliphaz from Teman,* Bildad from Shuh, and Zophar from Naamath. They met and journeyed together to give him sympathy and comfort. (Job 2:11)*

i. **A friend is someone who:**

b.*If the one falls, the other will help the fallen one. But woe to the solitary person! If that one should fall, there is no other to help. (Ecclesiastes 4:10)*

i. **'A   friend   is   someone   who:**

_____

_____

5. **Do you feel that you are friends with Jesus? List your top 3 reasons why.**
6. **What questions do you have about friendships, or about making friends?**

BIBLIOGRAPHY

Anonymous, *Catechism of the Catholic Church*, Libreria Editrice Vaticana, Vatican, 2000².

Anonymous, *Compendium of the Catechism of the Catholic Church*, United States Conference of Catholic Bishops, Washington, 2005.

Anonymous, *ECyDBook*, Mission Network USA, 2013 [Spanish Original published by Cantro de Estudios para la Adolescencia y la Juventud].

Bannon, Anthony LC, *Peter on the Shore*, Circle Press, Hamden, CT, 1996.

Blázquez, Jesús LC, *Dirección espiritual para los seglares [Spiritual Direction of Lay People]*, Legionarios de Cristo, Mexico City, 1994.

Clark, Chap, *Hurt 2.0: Inside the World of Today's Teenagers*, Baker Academic, Grand Rapids, MI, 2011.

Dubay, Thomas S.M., *Seeking Spiritual Direction: How to Grow the Divine Life Within*, St. Anthony Messenger Press, Cincinnati, 1993.

Epstein, Robert, *Teen 2.0: Saving Our Children and Families from the Torment of Adolescence*, Quill Driver Books, Fresno, CA, 2010.

Faber, Fr Frederick, *All for Jesus,* Sophia Institute Press, Manchester, NH, 2000.

Garrigou-Lagrange, Reginald O.P., *The Three Ages of the Interior Life: Prelude of Eternal Life,* TAN, Rockford, IL, 1989, 2 volumes.

Harris, Joshua, *I Kissed Dating Goodbye,* Multnomah Books, Sisters, OR, 1997.

John Paul II, *Christifideles Laici,* December 20, 1988.

John Paul II, *Familiaris Consortio,* November 22, 1981.

John Paul II, *Man and Woman He Created Them: A Theology of the Body,* Tr: Michael Waldstein, Pauline, Boston, MA, 2006.

John Paul II, *Pastores Dabo Vobis,* March 25, 1992.

Murray, David J. P., *genesis: Another chance for parents, educators, and anyone involved in education,* Circle press, Hamden, CT, 2007.

Philippe, Jacques, *Interior Freedom,* Scepter, New York, 2007.

Powell, Kara E., Griffin, Brad M., & Crawford, Cheryl A., *Sticky Faith, Youth Worker Edition: Practical Ideas to Nurture Long-Term Faith in Teenagers,* Zondervan, Grand Rapids, 2011.

Regnum Christi Consecrated Women, *Lecture Notes for the ECYD Guide Course,* unpublished, 2008.

Sentandreu, José García LC, *Adolescentes: guía en el caminar [Teens: a guidebook],* Centro Juvenil Puigmal, Barcelona, 2012³.

Tanquerey, Adolphe S.S., D.D, *The Spiritual Life: A Treatise on Ascetical and Mystical Theology,* Tr: The Rev. Herman Branders, S.S., A.M., First published by Desclee and Co., Tournai, Belgium, 130, photographic reproductions by TAN, Rockford, IL, 2000.

West, Christopher, *Theology of the Body Explained: A Commentary on John Paul II's "Gospel of the Body,"* Gracewing, Herefordshire, UK, 2003.

ABOUT THE AUTHOR

Fr Matthew P. Schneider graduated high school thinking of supporting a big family by designing computers, but God called him to be a religious and priest. He has directed youth ministry (groups, retreats, camps, and missions) in seven US states and three Canadian provinces. His studies include Engineering, Religious Studies, Classical Humanities, Philosophy, Theology, and specific studies regarding youth ministry. Since 2001 he has been a member of the Legionaries of Christ. Since 2007 he has been part of the product development team for Conquest Clubs and has written a significant portion of their material. He was ordained a priest in December 2013. He can be found in running around Canada or writing for *ProjectYM.com* on his channel *#22Catholic*. His writing has also been featured on *New Advent, BigPulpit.com, Catholic.net, Ignitium Today, Regnum Christi Live, CatholicismUSA, Spirit Daily,* and *Shalom Tidings*. He is very active on social media using the handle @FrMatthewLC.

CONQUEST AND CHALLENGE

Conquest and Challenge are comprehensive youth ministry programs for families, parishes and schools to help boys and girls know and love their Catholic faith, live Christian virtue and make a positive difference in the world around them. The programs are designed to instill virtue, develop character, and encourage spiritual growth all in a fun atmosphere of service, customized specifically for boys and girls respectively. The programs have been proven to be a successful youth ministry option for the past 10 years, present in over 300 parishes and schools across the USA and Canada.

The methodology is gender specific, team based, service driven and teen led. There are program materials offered for program adult leaders, teen leaders and members that include prayer books, calendar of saints and virtues, and T-shirts. Online training resources are also offered for program leadership and teen leaders.

The program curriculum is built from real questions that kids have at a specific ages about their faith, God, their friends, themselves and the world around them. Each weekly theme answers a question with a dynamic group activity, Gospel reflection and a story of a saint. The curriculum is offered in a series of virtue and project guidebooks, made for teens to lead teams of younger kids. Each guidebook has 8 weeks of activities and concludes with one apostolic service project.

www.conquestclubs.com / www.challengeclubs.com

ENDNOTES

1. Why Mentoring?

[1] The Pew Forum on Religion & Public Life, *Faith in Flux: Changes in Religious Affiliation in the U.S.*, April 27, 2009, http://www.pewforum.org/Faith-in-Flux.aspx.

[2] Cf. ROBERT EPSTEIN, *Teen 2.0: Saving Our Children and Families from the Torment of Adolescence,* Quill Driver Books, Fresno, CA, 2010.

[3] Cf. CLAUDIA WORRELL ALLEN & JOSEPH ALLEN, *Escaping Endless Adolescence: How We Can Help Our Teenagers Grow Up Before They Grow Old*, Ballantine, New York, 2009, Chapter 7: Hardwired to Connect.

[4] Cf. CHRISTIAN SMITH (with MELINDA LUNDQUIST DENTON), *Soul Searching: The Religious and Spiritual Lives of American Teenagers*, Oxford University Press, New York, Table 38. This only shows a relationship. From his study we have no way of telling if being able to turn to adults helped them be religious or by being religious they encountered more adults they could turn to.

[5] KARA E. POWELL, BRAD M. GRIFFIN & CHERYL A. CRAWFORD, *Sticky Faith, Youth Worker Edition: Practical Ideas to Nurture Long-Term Faith in Teenagers*, Zondervan, Grand Rapids, 2011, Kindle loc. 1113-1114.

[6] *Ibid*, Kindle loc. 2113-14.

7 Cf. DAVID KINNAMAN (with ALY HAWKINS), *You Lost Me: Why Young Christians Are Leaving Church … and Rethinking Faith*, Baker, Grand Rapids, MI, 2011, pg. 119. Although Kinnaman has evidently read Christian Smith, since he quotes him elsewhere, the conclusions I reference are based on his own studies.

8 Cf. CHAP CLARK, *Hurt 2.0: Inside the World of Today's Teenagers*, Baker Academic, Grand Rapids, MI, 2011. (This is an overarching theme of his whole book.)

9 The Pew Forum on Religion & Public Life, *Faith in Flux: Changes in Religious Affiliation in the U.S.*, April 27, 2009, http://www.pewforum.org/Faith-in-Flux.aspx (Note: The other factors not mentioned here [frequency at worship and a Catholic high school] show some divergence between the groups but are not nearly as definitive as the loss of faith as a teenager).

10 CHRISTIAN SMITH (with MELINDA LUNDQUIST DENTON), *Soul Searching: The Religious and Spiritual Lives of American Teenagers*, Oxford University Press, New York, pg 165.

11 Cf. ST. AUGUSTINE, *Confessions*, 3.6.11.

12 Cf. VATICAN II, *Gaudium et Spes*, #4.

13 JOHN PAUL II, *Christifideles Laici*, December 20, 1988, #58, emphasis added.

2. Where Does Mentoring Fit Into Comprehensive Youth Ministry?

1 Cf. KEITH R. ANDERSON & RANDY D. REESE, *Spiritual Mentoring: A Guide for Seeking and Giving Direction*, IVP Books, Downers Grove, IL 1999, pg 56.

2 It's a great read for all aspects of youth ministry. It's found at: http://www.usccb.org/about/laity-marriage-family-life-and-youth/young-adults/renewing-the-vision.cfm.

[3] At one point I considered writing this book as "Mentoring Teenagers" but I have never mentored a teenage girl and realized whatever explanation of their psychology I give would be inadequate.

[4] Quoted in: THOMAS DUBAY, S.M., *Seeking Spiritual Direction: How to Grow the Divine Life Within*, St. Anthony Messenger Press, Cincinnati, 1993, pg 276.

[5] I made up these titles to indicate types of books, they are not real titles.

[6] John 13:1.

[7] Hence Christ said, "Unless your righteousness exceeds that of the scribes and Pharisees, you will never enter the kingdom of heaven." (Matthew 5:20)

[8] CHRISTOPHER WEST, *Theology of the Body Explained: A Commentary on John Paul II's "Gospel of the Body,"* Gracewing, Herefordshire, UK, 2003, pg 236.

3. What is Mentoring?

[1] Cf. THOMAS DUBAY, S.M., *Seeking Spiritual Direction: How to Grow the Divine Life Within*, St. Anthony Messenger Press, Cincinnati, 1993, pg 275.

[2] Some people use spiritual direction for all forms of spiritual accompaniment. I am not necessarily opposed to that depending on what is understood by that, I just think failing to make this distinction causes confusion.

[3] Congregation for Catholic Education, *Pastoral Guidelines for Fostering Vocations to Priestly Ministry*, 25 March 2012, #4.

[4] Cf. JESÚS BLÁZQUEZ, LC, *Dirección espiritual para los seglares [Spiritual Direction of Lay People]*, Legionarios de Cristo, M;exico City, 1994, Chapter 2.

[5] Antonio Royo Marín, *Teología de la Perfección Cristiana [Theology of Christian Perfection]*, BAC 6th ed., Madrid, 1988, n.671, p.808, original translation.

[6] Thomas Dubay, S.M., *Seeking Spiritual Direction: How to Grow the Divine Life Within*, St. Anthony Messenger Press, Cincinnati, 1993, pg 96.

[7] For those unfamiliar with the four causes, take an example of a statue: it is made of wood or metal (material cause), in the shape of a person or animal (formal cause), by an artist (agent cause), so that you can admire it or to honor the person portrayed (final cause).

[8] In this book I will often use service projects and apostolates almost as synonyms: "service project" is a more common and more general term; "apostolate" refers to the action of an apostle, in other words a service project that is beyond simple humanitarianism.

[9] Thomas Dubay, S.M., *Seeking Spiritual Direction: How to Grow the Divine Life Within*, St. Anthony Messenger Press, Cincinnati, 1993, pg 61.

4. Who's Involved in Mentoring?

[1] *Compendium of the Catechism of the Catholic Church*, #146

[2] Tanquerey, Adolphe S.S., D.D, *The Spiritual Life: A Treatise on Ascetical and Mystical Theology*, Tr: The Rev. Herman Branders, S.S., A.M., First published by Desclee and Co., Tournai, Belgium, 130, photographic reproductions by TAN books, Rockford, IL, 2000, pg 51, #97.

[3] Cf. Isaiah 64:8.

[4] George Barna, *The Power of Vision: Discover and Apply God's Plan for Your Life and Ministry*, Regal, Ventura, CA, 2009, pg 95.

[5] Cf. John 15:16.

[6] Cf. John 14:26, 16:13.

[7] BENEDICT XVI, *World Youth Day 2005*, meeting with seminarians, August 19, 2005.

[8] FRANCIS DE SALES, *Introduction to the Devout Life*, John K. Ryan (tr), Image Books, New York, 1989, I.4, pg 47.

[9] Cf. LUIS MA. MENDIZÁBAL, *Dirección Espiritual*, BAC, Madrid, 1994, pgs. 72-73.

[10] Cf. ECyDBook, Mission Network USA, 2013, pg. 25-31.

5.   Where Does Mentoring Come From?
[1] Adapted from ABBA PAPHNUTIUS, *The Life of Saint Onuphrius, Hermit*, in *The Desert Fathers*, Book 1, Life 5, Chap. 1-3.

[2] Cf. Genesis 3:8.

[3] Exodus 33:11.

[4] Cf. Matthew 1:20, 2:13.

[5] Cf. 1 Samuel 3:1-19; Acts 10:1-22; Acts 9:8-20; Galatians 1:18-19.

[6] JOHN PAUL II, *Christifideles Laici*, December 20, 1988, #58, (emphasis mine).

6.   Teens Are Persons
[1] If you don't realize, the social worker is the one holding her little sister. The one with the arms outstretched is a English grammar and foreign languages teacher – and she gets excited about commas and exclamation points. The baby is still in University.

[2] Genesis 1:26.

[3] JACQUES PHILIPPE, *Interior Freedom*, Scepter, New York, 2007, pg

124.

[4] Having a faculty does not mean you have the capacity for every possible skill of that faculty. For example, I can speak but I lcan't speak poetic Vietnamese, or any Vietnamese for that matter, but I can speak poetic English if I try. Faculties need to developed and trained to reach their potential.

[5] ST. THOMAS AQUINAS, *Summa Contra Gentiles*, Vernon J. Bourke (tr), III, 90.6.

[6] VATICAN II, *Gaudium et Spes*, #22.

[7] JOHN PAUL II, *Veritatis Splendor*, #2.

[8] BENEDICT XVI, *Address at World Youth Day 2005*.

7. Adolescent Psychology

[1] CHIP CLARK, *Hurt 2.0: Inside the World of Today's Teenagers*, Baker Academic, Grand Rapids, MI, 2011, Kindle loc. 488.

[2] *Ibid*, Kindle loc. 499-501.

[3] Cf. *Ibid*, Chapter 1: the changing face of adolescence.

[4] Cf. ROBERT EPSTEIN, *Teen 2.0: Saving Our Children and Families from the Torment of Adolescence*, Quill Driver Books, Fresno, CA, 2010. (It is a repeated theme throughout the book involving various activities that would usually be considered teenager rebellion and various responsibilities.)

[5] Robert Epstein argues that this emotional roller-coaster is caused by western culture not nature. However, whether he is right or not is in some sense irrelevant to us. Mentoring is about changing boys not changing systems and I assume you will be mentoring boys in this culture.

[6] STEVEN REINBERG, "U.S. Kids Using Media Almost 8 Hours a Day," *Bloomberg Businessweek*, http://www.businessweek.com/lifestyle/content/healthday/635134. html.

[7] Cf. (whole paragraph) JOSHUA HARRIS, *I Kissed Dating Goodbye*, Multnomah Books, Sisters, OR, 1997.

[8] CHRISTOPHER WEST, *Theology of the Body Explained: A Commentary on John Paul II's "Gospel of the Body,"* Gracewing, Herefordshire, UK, 2003, pg 307.

[9] Matthew 5:28.

[10] For a positive presentation, Christopher West's *Theology of the Body for Teens* is probably the best book out there. Joshua Harris's *I Kissed Dating Goodbye* can also be useful but he comes from a protestant perspective and remains on the more practical level not bringing out the beauty of human sexuality as much.

[11] PJ DITTUS, J JACCARD, "Adolescents' perceptions of maternal disapproval of sex: relationship to sexual outcomes," *Journal of Adolescent Health* 2000;26:268-78.

[12] RICK NAUERT, "Relationship With Parents Influences Teen Drinking," *PsychCentral*, http://psychcentral.com/news/2009/04/24/relationship-with-parents-influences-teen-drinking/5515.html.

[13] Cf. CHRISTIAN SMITH (with MELINDA LUNDQUIST DENTON), *Soul Searching: The Religious and Spiritual Lives of American Teenagers*, Oxford University Press, New York, Kindle loc. 4612-13.

[14] Cf. (whole paragraph) JUDITH S. WALLERSTEIN, SANDRA BLAKESLEE, AND JULIA M. LEWIS, *The Unexpected Legacy of Divorce: A 25 Year Landmark Study*, Disney Books, 2000.

[15] Google "parent-teen relationship" and everything seems to be about communication – unfortunately the perspectives are wildly diverse and some clearly not in line with what we want to do.

8. Formation: Development of the Person's Dimensions

[1] These four areas are characteristic of ECyD and the name "Integral Formation" is copyrighted for related programs. A similar plan can be found in JOHN PAUL II, *Pastores Dabo Vobis*, 25 March 1992 although he applies these areas specifically to priestly rather than to youth formation. Other ways for dividing formation exist, but this one seems clearest to me. For example, the 8 components of youth ministry in *Renewing the Vision* seem to be similar.

[2] Camilleri Nozareno, *Principi di pedagogia cristiana* [*Principles of Christian Pedagogy*], (Torino: Marietti, 1960), p. 121, original translation.

[3] JOHN PAUL II, *Man and Woman He Created Them: A Theology of the Body*, Tr: MICHAEL WALDSTEIN, Pauline, Boston, MA, 2006, 15:1 pg 185.

9. Ten Pedagogical Principles

[1] Several sources, primarily: PAUL HARVEY, "The Rest of the Story," and JONANN BRADY & LEE FERRAN, "Turner: Tough Father 'Made Me a Better Man,'" http://abcnews.go.com/GMA/story?id=6222003.

[2] ST. THOMAS AQUINAS, *Commentary on the Sentences of Peter Lombard*, lib. 1 b2 q1 ad5, original translation.

[3] PIETRO BRAIDO, *La teoria dell'educazione e i suoi problemi* [*The Theory of Education and its Problems*], Pas-Verlag Roma, 1986, pg 17.

[4] Cf. TANQUEREY, ADOLPHE S.S., D.D, *The Spiritual Life: A Treatise on Ascetical and Mystical Theology*, TAN, Rockford, IL, 2000, pg 262, #541.

[5] Cf. DUBAY, THOMAS S.M., *Seeking Spiritual Direction: How to Grow the*

Divine Life Within, St. Anthony Messenger Press, Cincinnati, 1993, pg 107-8.

[6] *Didache* (the Teaching of the Twelve Apostles), 4:9, original translation.

[7] Cf. ORIGEN, *Contra Celsum [Origen Against Celsus]*, Book 4, Chap. 31.

[8] JOHN PAUL II, *Fides et Ratio*, September 14, 1998, #1 (emphasis in original).

[9] Cf. *Dedication and Leadership*, Douglas Hyde, Notre Dame Press, Notre Dame, IN.

[10] Luke 15:10.

[11] FR. JOHN A. HARDON, *The Catholic Catechism*, Part One: Doctrines of the Faith, IV. Jesus Christ, Pauline Christology, electronic version.

[12] *Ibid*, IV. Jesus Christ.

[13] John 15:5.

10. The Mentor's Role in Pedagogy

[1] Cf. CLAUDIA WORRELL ALLEN & JOSEPH ALLEN, *Escaping Endless Adolescence: How We Can Help Our Teenagers Grow Up Before They Grow Old*, Ballantine, New York, 2009, Chapter 6: Finding the Inner Adult & Chapter 7:Hardwired to Connect.

[2] Adapted from DAVID J. P. MURRAY, *genesis: Another chance for parents, educators, and anyone involved in education*, Circle press, Hamden, CT, 2007, pg 312.

[3] ROBERT EPSTEIN, *Teen 2.0: Saving Our Children and Families from the Torment of Adolescence*, Quill Driver Books, Fresno, CA, 2010, Chapter 6: Adultness.

[4] *Ibid*, Chapter 7: Young People Are Capable Thinkers.

[5] Cf. CLAUDIA WORRELL ALLEN & JOSEPH ALLEN, *Escaping Endless Adolescence: How We Can Help Our Teenagers Grow Up Before They Grow Old*, Ballantine, New York, 2009, Chapter 5: "It's a Good Thing I Was There!"

11. Introduction to the Spiritual Life for Teens

[1] FULTON J. SHEEN, *The Priest Is Not His Own*, Ignatius, San Francisco, 2005, pg 180.

[2] ST. AUGUSTINE, *Confessions*, Book 1, Chap. 1, original translation.

[3] 1 John 4:16.

[4] JOHN PAUL II, *Pastores Dabo Vobis*, March 25, 1992, #33.

[5] Cf. ST. THÉRÈSE OF LISIEUX, *Story of a Soul*, John C. Clark (tr), Institute of Carmelite Studies, Washington, 1996.

[6] Deuteronomy 30:19.

[7] *Catechism of the Catholic Church*, #2752.

[8] Many authors writing for a different audience give these stages a great importance and explanation. Reading either *The Spiritual Life: A Treatise on Ascetical and Mystical Theology* by Adolphe Tanquerey, or *The Three Ages of the Interior Life: Prelude of Eternal Life* by Reginald Garrigou-Lagrange. Both cover the entire spiritual life but neither is easy reading; Tanquery is shorter at 771 pages (that is saying something) but tends to be denser English. They agree on all key points but not always on emphasis or on a few disputed questions. I generally follow Tanquerrey more than Garigou-Lagrange but I respect both.

[9] ADOLPHE TANQUEREY, S.S., D.D, *The Spiritual Life: A Treatise on Ascetical and Mystical Theology*, TAN, Rockford, IL, 2000, pg 305, #636.

[10] THOMAS DUBAY, S.M., *Seeking Spiritual Direction: How to Grow the Divine Life Within*, St. Anthony Messenger Press, Cincinnati, 1993, pg 164-170.

[11] ST MAXIMILIAN KOLBE, *Aim Higher: Spiritual and Marian Reflections of St Maximilian Kolbe*, tr: Fr. Dominic Wisz, OFM CONV, Prow Books / Franciscan Marytown Press, Libertyville, IL, 1994, pg 17.

[12] ADOLPHE TANQUEREY, S.S., D.D, *The Spiritual Life: A Treatise on Ascetical and Mystical Theology*, TAN, Rockford, IL, 2000, pg 163-164, #321.

[13] John 12:24.

[14] ADOLPHE TANQUEREY, S.S., D.D, *The Spiritual Life: A Treatise on Ascetical and Mystical Theology*, TAN, Rockford, IL, 2000, pg 169, #335.'

12. Teenage Spiritual Principles

[1] Adapted from: ST JOHN BOSCO, *St. Dominic Savio*, Don Bosco Publications, New Rochelle, NY, pg 63-64.

[2] 1 Corinthians 13:1-5.

[3] COLUMBA MARMION, *Letter*, April 3, 1903 in *Union with God: Letters of Spiritual Direction by Blessed Columba Marmion*, ED: RAYMOND THIBAUT, TR: MOTHER MARY ST. THOMAS, Zaccheus Press, Bethesda, MD, 2006, pg 13.

[4] John 19:27.

[5] Cf. VATICAN II, *Lumen Gentium*, #10.

[6] 1 John 4:20.

[7] JOHN PAUL II, *Man and Woman He Created Them: A Theology of the Body*, Tr: MICHAEL WALDSTEIN, Pauline, Boston, MA, 2006, 14:4 pg

183.

[8] ST TERESA OF AVILA, *Interior Castle*, VI, 10.

13. Prayer
[1] 1 Thessalonians 5:17.

[2] Mark 14:38.

[3] CHARLES DE FOUCAULD, *Spiritual Autobiography of Charles de Foucauld*, Edited and Annotated by Jean-François Six, Translated by J. Holland Smith, Dimension Books, Denville, NJ, 1964, © 1964 P.J. Kenedy & Sons, New York, pg 85.

[4] *Catechism of the Catholic Church*, #2559.

[5] *Catechism of the Catholic Church*, #2558.

[6] *Catechism of the Catholic Church*, #2709, quoting St Thérèse of Lisieux.

[7] Matthew 18:20.

[8] Matthew 6:6.

[9] CHARLES DE FOUCAULD, *Spiritual Autobiography of Charles de Foucauld*, Edited and Annotated by Jean-François Six, Translated by J. Holland Smith, Dimension Books, Denville, NJ, 1964, © 1964 P.J. Kenedy & Sons, New York, pg 156.

[10] Quoted in DOM CHAUTARD, *The Soul of the Apostolate*, TAN, Rockford, IL 1977.

[11] FR FREDERICK FABER, *All for Jesus*, Sophia Institute Press, Manchester, NH, 2000, pg 77.

[12] ADOLPHE TANQUEREY, S.S., D.D, *The Spiritual Life: A Treatise on Ascetical and Mystical Theology*, TAN, Rockford, IL, 2000, pg 317, #657.

[13] *Ibid*, pg 311, #645 (emphasis in original).

[14] *Ibid*, pg 436, #920.

14. Specific Types of Prayer

[1] For example, the US Catholic bishops said Catholics should not practice Reiki. COMMITTEE ON DOCTRINE: UNITED STATES CONFERENCE OF CATHOLIC BISHOPS, *Guidelines for Evaluating Reiki as an Alternative Therapy*, 25 March 2009, http://old.usccb.org/doctrine/Evaluation_Guidelines_finaltext_2009-03.pdf

[2] *Catechism of the Catholic Church*, #1131.

[3] Examples: *Magnificat* (monthly subscription), *Daily Roman Missal* (all in one), *Novalis: Sunday Missal* (all in one each year), *St Joseph's Missal* (2 volume all in one).

[4] COLUMBA MARMIOM, *Letter*, March 7, 1907 in *Union with God: Letters of Spiritual Direction by Blessed Columba Marmion*, ED: RAYMOND THIBAUT, TR: MOTHER MARY ST. THOMAS, Zaccheus Press, Bethesda, MD, 2006, pg 25.

[5] JOHN PAUL II, *Dives in Misericordia*, November 30, 1980, #13.

[6] JACQUES PHILIPPE, *Interior Freedom*, Scepter, New York, 2007, pg 33.

[7] JOHN PAUL II, *Man and Woman He Created Them: A Theology of the Body*, Tr: MICHAEL WALDSTEIN, Pauline, Boston, MA, 2006, 65:3 pg 384.

[8] You can subscribe using on the following page: http://www.regnumchristi.org/english/listas/subscribe.phtml.

15. Content of Mentoring

[1] BARNA GROUP, *What People Experience in Churches*, January 9, 2012, http://www.barna.org/congregations-articles/556-what-people-

experience-in-churches. ("Practicing" means monthly attendance and saying your faith is important to you.)

2 Cf. JESÚS BLÁSQUEZ, *Dirección espiritual para los seglares [Spiritual Direction and Mentoring of the Laity]*, Legionarios de Cristo, Mexico City, 1996, pg 51-53.

16. Practical Suggestions

1 Cf. TANQUEREY, ADOLPHE S.S., D.D, *The Spiritual Life: A Treatise on Ascetical and Mystical Theology*, TAN, Rockford, IL, 2000, pg 99-101, #190-192.

2 J. ROBERT CLINTON & RICHARD W. CLINTON, "The Life Cycle of a Leader," in GEORGE BARNA (ED.), *Leaders on Leadership: Wisdom, Advice and Encouragement on the Art of Leading God's People*, Regal, Ventura, CA, 1997, pg 165 (emphasis in original).

3 LOUIS LALLEMANT, *La Doctrine spirituelle*, 4th principle, chap. 2, a. 2, pg. 187; translation: REGINALD GARRIGOU-LAGRANGE O.P., *The Three Ages of the Interior Life: Prelude of Eternal Life*, TAN, Rockford, IL, 1989, vol. 2 pg. 25. The original says "religious" not "mentors" but I am making its application here.

4 Cf. FRANK MERCADANTE, *Engaging a New Generation: A Vision for Reaching Catholic Teens*, Our Sunday Visitor, Huntingon, IN, 2012, pg 169-171. (This whole subsection is based off his talks and writings but this is the clearest reference. Frank Mercadante suggests organizing networks to make sure every teen in your parish is prayed for; this would be ideal but for this book I just focus on praying for the teens you mentor.)

5 DAVID J. P. MURRAY, *genesis: Another chance for parents, educators, and anyone involved in education*, Circle press, Hamden, CT, 2007, pg 70.

6THOMAS DUBAY, *Seeking Spiritual Direction, How to Grow the Divine Life Within*, St. Anthony Messenger Press, Cincinnati, Ohio, 1993, pg 33.

[7] *Compendium of the Catechism of the Catholic Church*, #150.

[8] JOHN BOSCO, *Scritti pedagogici e spirituali*, Rome, 1987, p. 294 (translation from: JOHN PAUL II, *Vita Consecrata: Post-Synodal Apostolic Exhortation*, March 25, 1996, #96)

[9] KARA E. POWELL, BRAD M. GRIFFIN & CHERYL A. CRAWFORD, *Sticky Faith, Youth Worker Edition: Practical Ideas to Nurture Long-Term Faith in Teenagers*, Zondervan, Grand Rapids, 2011, Kindle loc. 981-983.

[10] JOHN PAUL II, *Familiaris Consortio*, November 22, 1981, #36.

[11] *Catechism of the Catholic Church*, #2221.

[12] KARA E. POWELL, BRAD M. GRIFFIN & CHERYL A. CRAWFORD, *Sticky Faith, Youth Worker Edition: Practical Ideas to Nurture Long-Term Faith in Teenagers*, Zondervan, Grand Rapids, 2011, Kindle loc. 1147-1148.

[13] Make sure you do not conceive a teenage rebellion where he wants to be an adult with immaturity.

[14] Different mentors in different situations have to judge this differently. I am trying only to give you criteria to make a prudential judgment on each case in this paragraph. Working in the Midwest with teens who generally had good relationships with their parents, I would tend towards telling the parents in most cases. Another mentor I know who works in Europe told me he would almost never tell the parents.

17. Developing a Rule of Life

[1] ADOLPHE TANQUEREY, S.S., D.D, *The Spiritual Life: A Treatise on Ascetical and Mystical Theology*, TAN, Rockford, IL, 2000, pg 270-1, #559-560.

[2] Cf. Luke 14:28-33.

[3] Thomas à Kempis, *The Imitation of Christ*, Book I, Chap. 11 par. 5.

[4] John 3:30 (words of St John the Baptist).

[5] Cf. John 12:24.

[6] *Catechism of the Catholic Church*, #1022; St John of the Cross, *Complete Works, Dichos [Sayings]*, 64; Cf. Matthew 25:31-46.

18. Generosity and Vocations

[1] Cf. John 4:1-42 (several quotes from this passage are in this section).

[2] Cf. Mathew 13:3-23 (3-8 quoted), Mark 4:3-20, Luke 8:5-15.

[3] Center for Applied Research in the Apostolate, *The Class of 2011: Survey of Ordinands to the Priesthood*, Washington, DC, 2011, pg. 20, http://www.usccb.org/beliefs-and-teachings/vocations/ordination-class/upload/ordination-class-2011-report.pdf.

[4] Anthony Bannon LC, *Vocation: questions & answers*, Circle Press, Hamden, CT, 2004, pg 123.

[5] *Idem.*

[6] *Idem.*

[7] John 15:16.

[8] Matthew 11:30.

[9] Center for Applied Research in the Apostolate, *The Class of 2011: Survey of Ordinands to the Priesthood*, Washington, DC, 2011, pg. 4, http://www.usccb.org/beliefs-and-teachings/vocations/ordination-class/upload/ordination-class-2011-report.pdf.

[10] Anthony Bannon LC, *Peter on the Shore*, Circle Press, Hamden,

CT, 1996, pg 161.

19. Some Closing Thoughts

[1] Cf. ST AUGUSTINE, *Confessions*, 4:2. (Obviously he had a mistress before he converted.)

[2] GREGORY THE GREAT, *Past.*, p. 1 c. 1, quoted in ALPHONSUS DE LIGOURI, *Duties and Dignities of the Priest*, Ed: EUGENE GRIMM, Redemptorist Fathers, Brooklyn, 1927, pg. 273.

[3] FR FREDERICK FABER, *All for Jesus*, Sophia Institute Press, Manchester, NH, 2000, pg 89.

Appendix A: The Four Qualities of a Mentor

[1] Cf. JIM COLLINS, *Good to Great: Why Some Companies Make the Leap… and Others Don't*, HarperBusiness, New York, 2001, pg. 20.

Appendix C: 99 Simple Resolutions

[1] David Murray let me copy most of this appendix from: DAVID J. P. MURRAY, *genesis: Another chance for parents, educators, and anyone involved in education*, Circle press, Hamden, CT, 2007, pg. 335-343. I have changed some parts of it since we are dealing with youth ministry while his list is for a school.

Appendix D: A Model Guide Sheet

[1] I got this guide sheet from Br Lucio Boccacci, LC who has developed this method most of the mentors I know personally. He has developed several that he has available for free on his blog youth2change.com.